Cries from the Cross

BOOKS IN THE PROTESTANT PULPIT EXCHANGE

Cries from the Cross

Sermons on the Seven Last Words of Jesus

Leighton Farrell

PROTESTANT
PULPIT
EXCHANGE

Abingdon Press
Nashville

CRIES FROM THE CROSS:
SERMONS ON THE SEVEN LAST WORDS OF JESUS

Copyright © 1994 by Abingdon Press

This book is printed on acid-free, recycled paper.

FARRELL, LEIGHTON, 1930–
    Cries from the cross : sermons on the seven last words of Jesus / Leighton Farrell.
        p.   cm. — (Protestant pulpit exchange)
    ISBN 0-687-13296-7 (alk. paper)
    1. Jesus Christ—Seven last words—Sermons.   2. Easter—Sermons.
3. Lenten sermons.   4. Sermons, American.   I. Title.   II. Series.
BT456.F37   1994   93-41820
232.96'35—dc20

Unless otherwise noted, scripture quotations are from the New Revised Standard Version of the Bible, copyright © 1989 by the Division of Christian Education of the National Council of the Churches of Christ in the USA. Used by permission.

Those noted JBP are from *The New Testament in Modern English*, Revised Ed., by J. B. Phillips. Copyright © 1972 by J. B. Phillips. Used by permission of Macmillan Publishing Co..

94 95 96 97 98 99 00 01 02 03 — 10 9 8 7 6 5 4 3 2 1

MANUFACTURED IN THE UNITED STATES OF AMERICA

Contents

Preface

This book is composed of sermons preached on the "seven last words of Jesus from the cross" to the congregation of Highland Park United Methodist Church in Dallas, Texas, during the Lenten Season of 1992. I have also included sermons preached on Easter Sunday, 1992, and Easter Sunday, 1993. I have attempted to consider the events surrounding the "seven last words of Jesus from the cross" from the viewpoint of the participants in relation to the Crucifixion. This, at times, calls for conjecture on my part, meaning that I have taken great historical liberty concerning those persons and events. It is hoped that the sermons will be read with that concept in mind.

I am greatly indebted to many keen minds and great spirits for ideas, thoughts, concepts, directions, and illustrations. Throughout the years I have listened to, and read sermons from, the pulpit masters of this and other days, and many of their ideas have become a part of my own thoughts. I trust that I have not borrowed too heavily from any of them without permission.

I am grateful to my beloved wife, Julie, who encouraged me to write these sermons; to the faithful members of Highland Park United Methodist Church, who have listened to my sermons over the last twenty years with such attentive and responsive hearts; to my secretary, Lila Foree, for cheerfully carrying an extra burden; to all of those who have contributed to my thought in the development of these sermons—but especially to the One who said, "Father, forgive them."

Leighton Farrell
Dallas, Texas

Introduction

Throughout the centuries the cross has stood at the center of the Christian faith. Why? Because it reveals to us the great love God has for God's people.

The cross still stands at the center of our faith today, revealing anew the saving grace of God. The power of the cross has not diminished through the ages. The cross is the eternal symbol of God's love. The cross reveals to us our sinfulness and God's forgiveness; our need and God's grace. The cross gives us the assurance of God's forgiving love as we seek to do God's will as the people of God.

We see pain and suffering, anguish and sorrow in the world. We realize the magnitude of the problems and we recognize our incompetence to solve them. We cry out, "My God, my God, why have you forsaken us?" or "Where is God in the midst of the world's pain?" or "Why doesn't God do something about the problem?" And the answer is: God *has* done something about it.

"For God so loved the world that he gave his only Son, so that everyone who believes in him may not perish but may have eternal life." (John 3:16)

He who did not withhold his own Son, but gave him up for all of us, will he not with him also give us everything else? (Rom. 8:32)

But God proves his love for us in that while we still were sinners Christ died for us. (Rom. 5:8)

Throughout the ages the Christian church has found strength, courage, and hope in what we call "the seven last words" of Jesus from the cross. As used here, *word* means a brief statement rather than a single unit of letters. As we study the seven last words (statements) of Jesus from the cross, we see God's power in action, both then and now. Fewer than fifty words in all, these seven brief statements reveal to us what was most important to Jesus in the final hours of his life on earth. His last words were not those of a cowed, beaten person who was afraid of death. These were the words of a brave soul who knew that death was near, yet found the strength in those critical final minutes to say to those who were around him the things that were important to him.

The seven last words of Jesus from the cross are not readily discernible. They are not neatly placed together, listed one after another, in any one of the Gospels. Yet each Gospel contains at least one of the seven last words.

Matthew and Mark contain only one of the words: "My God, my God, why have you forsaken me?" Luke has three of the seven last words: "Father, forgive them; for they do not know what they are doing"; "Truly I tell you, today you will be with me in Paradise"; and "Father, into your hands I commend my spirit." These three words are found only in the Gospel of Luke. John has recorded three words not found in any of the other Gospels: "Woman, here is your

Son. . . . Here is your mother"; "I am thirsty"; and "It is finished."

The order in which Christ's words are discussed here is my own preference, and does not represent any ordained sequence. It is only by combining the stories from the four Gospels that we see a complete picture of the Crucifixion and hear the seven last words of Jesus from the cross. If we had only one Gospel story of the Crucifixion, we would have less than a complete story of Jesus' last hours.

But the story is not finished with the Incarnation and the cross—the final victory belongs to God. The Resurrection must be added to the story. The Incarnation, the cross, and the Resurrection must be brought together until we see them as one divine act of God. The story of Christ is the story of God intervening in history for the salvation of the world. For the Christian this means that for every Good Friday there is an Easter morning; for every crucifixion there is a resurrection. There can be triumph over every tragedy life brings to us, and where God is, the forces of evil will never have the final word. We rejoice in the promise of scripture:

> "Death has been swallowed up
> in victory."
> "Where, O death, is your
> victory?
> Where, O death, is your
> sting?"

The sting of death is sin, and the power of sin is the law. But thanks be to God, who gives us the victory through our Lord Jesus Christ. (1 Cor. 15:54b-57)

Cries from the Cross

First Word

Two others also, who were criminals, were led away to be put to death with him. When they came to the place that is called The Skull, they crucified Jesus there with the criminals, one on his right and one on his left. Then Jesus said, "Father, forgive them; for they do not know what they are doing."
(Luke 23:32-34)

"Father, forgive them. . . ."

A centurion, a hard-bitten soldier of the Roman guard, stood in the shadow of the cross. He was responsible for overseeing the crucifixions that day. He looked up at the men on the crosses. The man on the center cross had been his constant companion since the early hours of the morning. The centurion had taken him to Pilate. He watched as Pilate exonerated himself of any responsibility for this man.

On the day of the Crucifixion the centurion was in charge of the grim procession up the hill to Golgotha. The centurion had seen many men die on the cross. Death was no stranger to him. He was not easily touched by suffering or pain; he was not readily moved by sorrow or anguish.

But this day the centurion had seen something different about the way this man called Jesus responded to his suffering—something that the centurion could recognize as the qualities of love and steadfastness and composure.

This day the centurion heard something different from what he was accustomed to hearing from a man suffering on a cross. He heard Jesus say, "Father, forgive them." These words were unexpected—words of reconciliation and healing. I wonder, given the limits of our finite understanding, if we can ever know the heights and depths of those words.

> *"A cry for mercy . . . that would have been the cry of an ordinary person."*

A crucifixion was the most horrible and degrading of all deaths that could come to anyone, designed to humiliate as well as to kill. Death on the cross was not an instant death; it was a long, lingering, suffering death. Roman citizens were never crucified. Crucifixion was reserved for slaves and criminals and the lowest of people. Jesus was obviously considered in this category, among the lowest of the low. Yet, in the midst of all this he was able to say, "Father, forgive them."

That must have been what caught the attention of the centurion. The words were so out of character for the event. An oath demanding retribution, a curse on those who hanged him there—that is what the centurion expected from someone on the cross. Or a cry for mercy—a cry for the swift release of death—that would have been the cry of an ordinary person. But in the midst of the horrors of crucifixion, for someone to forgive and pray for others—that was not the manner of ordinary people. A person on the cross does not normally pray, "Father, forgive them."

It was this same remembrance that stayed with Jesus' disciples through the years. It became a part of who they were, and a part of their whole life. Years later Peter wrote his thoughts on the cross and said, "When he was abused, he did not return abuse; when he suffered, he did not threaten; but he entrusted himself to the one who judges justly" (1 Pet. 2:23). The apostle Paul wrote that he could never understand the depth of the cross. He wrote that if people had been lovable, kind, understanding, and worthy, then Jesus' prayer might have made sense to him. But that Christ could forgive those who crucified him, pray for and die for his enemies, that was not the manner of people.

"In human experience," the Phillips translation of the New Testament tells us, "it is a rare thing for one man to give his life for another, even if the latter be a good man, though there have been a few who have had the courage to do it. Yet the proof of God's amazing love is this: that it was while we were sinners that Christ died for us" (Rom. 5:7, 8 JBP).

> *"Forgiveness doesn't keep score."*

Why would Jesus be willing to pray from the cross, "Father, forgive them"? Why would he be willing to give up his life for people who didn't even like him? Judged by human standards there was no reason why he should. Search for parallels— there are none. There are a few instances of persons who died gallantly for their faith. Young Stephen was stoned to death for his beliefs. The early church martyrs died bravely and courageously for their faith. The Bible translators suffered and died for their convictions. Stephen and the early church martyrs and the Bible translators and all those through the years who have given themselves for others learned that self-giving love from the one who said, "Father, forgive them."

On one occasion Peter asked Jesus, "Master, how many times can my brother wrong me and I must forgive him? Would seven be enough?" "No," replied Jesus, "not seven times, but seventy times seven!"

Peter said seven times because he thought that would be

more than enough. Jesus said "seventy times seven," not to make it 490 times, but to make certain that Peter saw that forgiveness doesn't keep score! Jesus wanted to be certain that Peter understood that all the forgiveness we give to others is infinitesimal compared with the immeasurable grace of God.

Then Jesus told a parable to illustrate forgiving others. He said, "The kingdom of heaven may be compared to a king who wished to settle accounts with his slaves" (Matt. 18:23).

One of the slaves was found to owe the king ten thousand talents—a tremendous amount of money! Even one talent was a considerable amount. The total annual taxes of Judea, Idumea, Samaria, Galilee, and Perea, all added together, amounted to only eight hundred talents. And all the gold used in the ark of the covenant was worth less than thirty talents. One talent was worth about two thousand dollars in 1993 U.S. dollars, or the equivalent of fifteen years' wages for a laborer in Jesus' day. Ten thousand talents would be equivalent to two million dollars. Obviously, Jesus was making the point that the man owed more than he could ever repay in many lifetimes.

The king was alarmed at the amount of debt that the servant owed. The man was brought to the king and "as he could not pay, his lord ordered him to be sold, together with his wife and children and all his possessions, and payment to be made" (Matt. 18:25).

The servant fell down before the king and begged, "Have patience with me, and I will pay you everything" (Matt. 18:26). The king was moved with pity for the servant, set him free and canceled the debt. In our better moments we recognize ourselves as helpless debtors standing in the presence of God who says to us, "Forgiven!"

The servant who had been forgiven so much left the court of the king and in the courtyard met a fellow servant who owed him one hundred denarii. One denarius was worth about twenty cents or the equivalent of one day's wage for a laborer. One hundred denarii was about twenty dollars in 1993 U.S. dollars. The forgiven servant grabbed the servant who owed him one hundred denarii and said, "Pay what you owe" (Matt. 18:28). The man fell at his fellow servant's feet and begged him, "Have patience with me, and I will pay you" (Matt. 18:29), but he refused and had him jailed until he would pay the debt.

> *"All of God's mercy is wasted on us unless we become merciful persons."*

Though the servant who owed a large debt was forgiven of that debt by the king, and though the servant who owed a small debt pleaded his case in identical words, the forgiven servant was not a forgiving servant!

When the king heard about this event, he called the forgiven servant and said, "I forgave you all that debt because you pleaded with me. Should you not have had mercy on your fellow slave, as I had mercy on you?" (Matt. 18:32*b*-33). Then he cast the unforgiving servant into prison.

I believe that Jesus told this parable to emphasize that we who are not forgiving persons have a difficult time being forgiven; that we have no kinship with the Father unless we possess the Father's spirit; and that all of God's mercy is wasted on us unless we become merciful persons.

Do not mistake the teaching here: God's love is not conditional; God's forgiveness is not conditional. What Jesus is teaching is that we are not prepared to accept forgiveness from God until our hearts are forgiving toward others. Until we confess and repent of our own sins, which include the sins of hatred, resentment, and a lack of love for one another, God's forgiveness cannot become effective in our hearts.

In *The Merchant of Venice,* Shakespeare writes:

> Though justice be thy plea, consider this,
> That in the course of justice none of us
> Should see salvation: we do pray for mercy,
> And that same prayer doth teach us all to render
> The deeds of mercy.
>
> (*The Merchant of Venice,* act 5, sc. 1)

The heart of the New Testament teaching about forgiving others is this: our right to ask for the forgiveness of God is fair insofar as we are willing to apply the same principle of forgiveness to all those with whom we deal day by day.

Jesus said, "Father, forgive them."

There was a man whose family had major conflicts, turmoils, and misunderstandings for years. Many members of the family did not speak to one another. There was conflict over business, money, and power. One day one of the brothers in that family heard his minister read Jesus' words from the Sermon on the Mount. One particular section struck him as if he had never heard it before: "So when you are offering your gift at the altar, if you remember that your brother or sister has something against you, leave your gift there before the altar and go; first be reconciled to your brother or sister, and then come and offer your gift" (Matt. 5:23-24).

Immediately the man went to one of his brothers who had been estranged from the family for many years, and sought reconciliation. It did not come quickly or easily. It took months of forgiving and years of healing to bring the family together. It only happened when the reconciling brother took seriously Jesus' words: "Father, forgive them."

In our better moments we almost understand that the only way we can learn to live together is to forgive. In our better moments we almost comprehend the love of God in Christ. In our better moments we almost believe that love is the greatest thing in the world. In our better moments we almost understand what Jesus meant when he said, "Father, forgive them."

What is there in that single, solitary figure, hanging on the cross, praying that God will forgive his enemies, that makes us want to forgive our enemies? What is there that makes us feel that this dying man on the cross was an act of God that involves and includes all of us down through the centuries? What is there about the words, "Father, forgive them," that haunts us yet today?

Is it that we know we have not yet had the compassion to forgive those who have wronged us? Is it that we know we do not yet have the courage to go to those who have wronged us and begin the process of reconciliation? Is it that we know that we do not yet have the spirit of forgiving love to overcome the dreadful bitterness we harbor because of the wrongs done to us? The first words from the cross are haunting, judging words, "Father, forgive them." They haunt us still.

Martin Niemöller was a German Lutheran pastor of great prominence during the 1930s when Hitler was rising to power in the Nazi party. From the very beginning Niemöller saw what Hitler was and what he had in mind for Germany. Niemöller became a leader in the anti-Nazi movement and spoke against the Nazi party on every occasion he could. Because of this activity he was arrested and placed in a Nazi concentration camp, where he was Hitler's special prisoner. Day after day he watched the prison guards mistreat the prisoners, and he pondered the words of Jesus on the cross, "Father, forgive them." He did not see how such an act of forgiveness could be humanly possible.

> ## "God is not the enemy of my enemies."

When he was released from the concentration camp Martin Niemöller wrote about his inner struggle during his eight years of confinement. He said that he was grateful that he was not released sooner because it was during the latter part of his imprisonment that he learned what Jesus really meant when he said: "Father, forgive them."

Outside Niemöller's cell window at Dachau, a gallows had been set up. He could see it day after day as other prisoners were put to death. He could hear their prayers and their curses. "That gallows," he wrote, "became my most reliable teacher. There were questions in the back of my mind: What will happen, Martin Niemöller, on the day they lead you out there and put you to the test? When they put that rope around your neck, what will be your last words? Will you cry out, 'You criminals, you scum, there's a God in heaven, you'll get yours.' Or, will you be able to say with Jesus, 'Father, forgive them'?"

What would you say? What would I say? I don't know. Martin Niemöller went on to write, "It took me a long time to learn that God is not the enemy of my enemies. In fact, He is not even the enemy of His enemies."

God turns enemies into friends by forgiving them, loving them, and saving them. They cried out, "He saved others, he cannot save himself. Let him come down from the cross now and we will believe in him." Jesus simply said, "Father, forgive them."

Could I, while being stoned to death for my beliefs, say, "Father, forgive them"? Could I, while being mauled by the lions in the coliseum, say, "Father, forgive them"? Could I, while being burned at the stake for translating the Bible so that all could read it, say, "Father, forgive them"? I don't know. Could you?

We do not have to face being stoned to death or mauled by the lions or burned at the stake. But we do have to face the question, "Can we overcome the hurt caused by the injustices and wrongs done to us, reach out in reconciling love, and pray with Jesus, 'Father, forgive them'?"

Second Word

> *One of the criminals who were hanged there kept deriding him and saying, "Are you not the Messiah? Save yourself and us!" But the other rebuked him, saying, "Do you not fear God, since you are under the same sentence of condemnation? And we indeed have been condemned justly, for we are getting what we deserve for our deeds, but this man has done nothing wrong." Then he said, "Jesus, remember me when you come into your kingdom." He replied, "Truly I tell you, today you will be with me in Paradise."*
> *(Luke 23:39-43)*

"Today you will be with me in Paradise."

The criminals who hung on the crosses on either side of Jesus were in all probability vicious, cold-blooded, heartless men, who had no concern for honesty or fairness or truth. On the center cross they saw the third victim of crucifixion, and his calmness of spirit invoked their contempt.

They joined with the mob in hurling taunts and jeers at him, saying with them, "Aha! You who would destroy the temple and build it in three days, save yourself, and come down from the cross! In the same way the chief priests, along with the scribes, were also mocking him among themselves and saying, 'He saved others; he cannot save himself. Let the Messiah, the King of Israel, come down from the cross now, so that we may see and believe'" (Mark 15:29*b*-32*a*).

Jesus suffered abuse, insults, and mistreatment, yet he spoke no word of complaint. Only compassion and sympathy were expressed on his face. From a heart filled with grief and pain, he prayed, "Father, forgive them." Almost at once a definite change came over one of the thieves who had been hurling taunts at Jesus. Something happened that caused him to see that this was no ordinary man. This was not the face of a criminal, his acts were not the acts of a hardened man. The thief became convinced that Jesus was innocent of any crime.

Speaking to his companion in crime, the thief said, "Aren't you afraid of God, even when you are getting the same punishment as he is? And it is fair enough for us, as we have only got what we deserve, but this man never did anything wrong in his life." And then he said, "Jesus, remember me when you come into your kingdom." And Jesus answered, "I tell you, this day you will be with me in paradise."

> *"There is nothing in the world so tenacious and resolute as the grace of God."*

Fascinating story, isn't it? Most of us would like to say, "Why did God save the thief on the cross who only repented moments before his death? Why did God want to save him? It doesn't seem fair that the thief on the cross received the same grace as those who had been faithful all their lives!"

A lot of what God has done throughout history hasn't seemed fair to people. Why was Jacob not denounced by God for his conniving ways? Why was David not disowned by God for his disgraceful actions? Why was the adulteress not condemned by Jesus for her open disregard of the moral laws? Why was Peter not disavowed by God after his blatant denial of Christ in the courtyard? Why was Paul not banished by God forever because of his persecution of the Christians early in his life? Why? That is the question: Why? And the answer is because there is nothing in the world so tenacious and resolute as the grace of God. The Gospel of John tells us: "God did not send the Son into the world to condemn the world, but in order that the world might be saved through him" (John 3:17).

The Bible does not condone Jacob's wily ways or David's premeditated sin or the adulteress' actions or Peter's denial or Paul's persecution of Christians. But it does take those tragic events and work them into the final pattern of God's will for the world. Where would any of us be if it were not for the infinite patience of a loving God? Where would we find hope were it not for the forgiving, reconciling grace of God?

If we were honest with ourselves, we would admit that God ought to have given up on us long ago. Remembering our defeats in the face of temptation, our compromises with evil, and our unreliability in spiritual matters, we realize how far we have come from where God wants us to be. God ought to have given up on us—but God has not. Why? Because of God's infinite, patient love; because of God's tenacious, resolute grace.

Jesus taught his disciples a parable, saying, "The kingdom of heaven is like a landowner who went out early in the morning to hire laborers for his vineyard" (Matt. 20:1). The landowner found a few who wanted to work, and he promised them each a silver coin for the day's work. About nine o'clock he returned to the marketplace to hire some more workers, promising to pay them a fair wage for their work. He went back at noon and at three o'clock in the afternoon and hired more workers and promised them fair pay. Then at the eleventh hour, or about five o'clock, with the shadows lengthening, he hired more workers.

At sunset the landowner directed his foreman to pay the workers, beginning with those who were hired last and ending with those who were hired first. To their surprise, those who were hired last received a silver coin, the equivalent of a full day's wage. Those who worked three, six, or nine hours were also paid a full day's wage. Finally, the time came to pay those who had worked the full day. Those workers saw how generous the landowner had been with those who had worked for less than a full day, and they assumed that they would get more than a day's wage. But they received only what had been promised—a silver coin.

> ## "How hard our doctrine of merit dies!"

Those who worked all day grumbled at the landowner and said, "These last worked only one hour, and you have made them equal to us who have borne the burden of the day and the scorching heat" (Matt. 20:12). It may have been that it was not so much that those who had worked the full day wanted more money, for they received what they had been promised; it may have been that they felt that those who worked fewer hours deserved less pay.

In this parable the lovelessness of the longtime workers is set in contrast to the love of God. How hard our doctrine of merit dies! How proud we are of our good works! How blindly we offer our legalities in protest against God's free grace! How loveless we are toward the sinner who repents at the last moment!

The landowner turned to one of the disgruntled ones and said, "Friend, I am doing you no wrong; did you not agree with me for the usual daily wage? Take what belongs to you and go; I choose to give to this last the same as I give to you. Am I not allowed to do what I choose with what belongs to me? Or are you envious because I am generous?" (Matt. 20:13-15).

In this parable each laborer, no matter how long he worked, received the same pay. This is not a parable about economics; it is a parable about God's grace. This is a parable about God and God's people. It teaches us that God is free to bestow gifts upon us as he chooses! God has chosen to bestow love and grace upon us: undeserved, unmerited, and unearned by us.

This parable speaks not of the kingdom of this world; it speaks of the kingdom of God and God's love for us. God's saving grace has nothing to do with our years of service or our good works. How hard it is for us to give up our doctrine of good works!

The dying thief was just as well off as a person who had been a believer for many years. The prodigal son who returned home was received with as much love as the older brother who stayed at home and worked from dawn to dark. The sinner who comes to God at the eleventh hour is just as blessed as the one who comes at the beginning of the day. We are forgiven by God's grace—not by good works or sound doctrine, not by education or wealth, not by prestige or power—we are forgiven by God's grace.

It is interesting to note that throughout the teachings of the New Testament the rewards of God are not according to human standards of judgment. Nowhere in the ministry of Jesus is this more clearly revealed than in his conversation with the penitent thief on the cross. Whenever Jesus talked with a person he assumed that God was working in that person's life. And it didn't matter whether that person was respectable or not, whether that person was accepted in the synagogue or not—that person was loved by God. This is the gospel. This is the good news. Not our good works, but God's grace. God's forgiveness came to the penitent thief not when he denied his guilt, but when he acknowledged the justice of the punishment given him. "And we indeed have been condemned justly, for we are getting what we deserve for our deeds" (Luke 23:41).

> "God's grace is the love that destroys all our pride."

Some of the most striking stories in the New Testament involve the failure of people and the grace of God. Simon, the Pharisee, invited Jesus to his home to eat with him. A woman in the city, who was a sinner, went to Simon's home and stood behind Jesus. She bathed his feet with her tears, wiped them dry with her hair, and anointed them with ointment. It seems obvious that she was repenting of her sins. Jesus said to her, "Your sins are forgiven. . . . Your faith has saved you" (Luke 7:48-50). How wonderful is God's grace!

On another occasion Jesus was teaching in the Temple and the scribes and Pharisees brought a woman caught in adultery before the assembly. In order to test Jesus they said, "In the law Moses commanded us to stone such women. Now what do you say?" (John 8:5). Jesus replied, "Let anyone among you who is without sin be the first to throw a stone at her" (John 8:7). When they heard this word, they silently filed out of the Temple. Jesus said to the woman, "'Has no one condemned you?' She said, 'No one, sir.' And Jesus said, 'Neither do I condemn you. Go your way and from now on do not sin again'" (John 8:10, 11). How wonderful is God's grace!

> "If God's judgments were as harsh as our judgments, no one could be saved."

We are saved by God's grace. This grace is the love that destroys all our pride. As children of the Reformation we understand that we do not earn our salvation. We have given up good works as a means of redemption. We confess our sins; we ask for God's forgiveness; we accept God's grace. For if the man who came to work at 5:00 P.M. did not earn his wage, neither did the man who was in the vineyard early. Once we understand this, there is no more foolish talk about who deserves a silver coin and who does not. If God's judgments were as harsh as our judgments, no one could be saved.

Bishop Emerson Colaw writes that during one Lenten season he went to see a drama that portrayed the life of Jesus. *The Man Born to Be King* reached its climax in the Crucifixion scene. The three Marys entered and approached the Roman guards. Mary, the mother of Jesus, spoke to the captain requesting permission to minister to the needs of her son. He roughly pushed her away. Then one of the other women came forward and sought permission, adding, "For old times' sake." The captain refused her request also. Then with a sweeping motion of her hand she loosed her golden hair so that it could cascade down her back. "Marcellus," she asked, "have you ever seen hair like this?" And then she thrust out a foot and asked, "And have feet ever danced for you like these feet?"

Incredulity was on his face. In amazement he said,

"Mary Magdalene, how you have changed!" Slowly, with dramatic emphasis, she turned so that her back was to the audience and she was facing Christ on the cross and slowly said, "Yes, Marcellus, I have changed; he changed me!"

That is what repentance and forgiveness and grace are all about: "He changed me." From the thief on the cross to Mary Magdalene to the apostle Paul to St. Augustine to Joan of Arc to people who are struggling to overcome sin in their lives today, that is what grace is all about.

We begin to understand something about the conversation between Jesus and the penitent thief on the cross when we begin to understand something about God's grace.

Third Word

> *Meanwhile, standing near the cross of Jesus were his mother, and his mother's sister, Mary the wife of Clopas, and Mary Magdalene. When Jesus saw his mother and the disciple whom he loved standing beside her, he said to his mother, "Woman, here is your son." Then he said to the disciple, "Here is your mother." And from that hour the disciple took her into his own home.*
> *(John 19:25-27)*

"Here is your son. . . . Here is your mother."

Jesus looked down from the agony of the cross and saw his mother standing near the foot of the cross. He saw her haunted look. He saw the tears in her eyes. He saw the desolation in her face. When Jesus saw his mother, it must have stirred within him memories of Nazareth: the home she had made for him, the love she had lavished on him, and the concern with which she had followed every stage of his life and ministry.

His thoughts of the past must have brought thoughts of the future and what would happen after he died. What makes death so difficult for so many is not the thought of dying but the thought of those who are left behind. What will become of them? Who will watch over them? Who will care for them? What will they do when the one who has loved and cared for them is gone?

In the agony of dying, Jesus was aware of the needs of his mother and made provision for her. The scripture tells us that standing beside Mary was her nephew, her son's closest friend, John. (Salome, the mother of the sons of Zebedee, was also at the cross and may have been Mary's sister.) To his mother Jesus said, "Woman, here is your son" (John 19:26). And to John he said, "Here is your mother" (John 19:27). From that hour, the scripture tells us, John took Mary into his own home.

Why did Jesus entrust Mary to John, the beloved disciple, and not to his own brothers? It would have been natural for Jesus to have entrusted Mary to her own family. The common response would have been: "Mother, your other sons will take care of you after my death." But that is not what Jesus said.

Why did Jesus not request that one of her own sons, one of his own brothers, James or Joseph or Judas or Simon, take care of their mother? The answer is supplied in a terse comment in the Gospel of John, "For not even his brothers believed in him" (John 7:5). "Prophets," Jesus said at an earlier time, "are not without honor except in their own country and in their own house" (Matt. 13:57). And Jesus spoke about this from firsthand experience. The members of his own family were not yet disciples. They had not accepted his claims or believed in his mission. After the Resurrection, the scriptures tell us, his brothers *were* found among the disciples, and one of them, James, became the leader of the church in Jerusalem. But at the time of the Crucifixion, Jesus entrusted Mary to John, because he was a devoted disciple, one who was in complete sympathy with Jesus and his mission.

It is not surprising that Jesus was misunderstood by his family. It is not surprising that they didn't believe in him. It is not surprising that they believed him to be a misguided person. Jesus has been misunderstood for almost two thousand years.

> *"Others mistook Jesus for a miracle man."*

The realists of his day mistook him for an ambitious revolutionary upstart who threatened their position, power, and prestige and as one who must be banished. The Pharisees and chief priests mistook him for a misguided reformer who might undermine the whole religious system and upset the power structure that they had created. The zealots mistook him for the deliverer who would free them from the bondage of Rome by setting up an earthly kingdom. They thought he would come as the Messiah leading an army and taking over the Roman government. Still others mistook Jesus for a miracle man who would provide them with food, clothing, shelter, and security.

> *"Today, we still misunderstand Jesus."*

His own close friends also misunderstood him. Peter thought Jesus' role and destiny would preclude any possibility of his submitting to a cross, but it did not. James and John thought that Jesus would inaugurate a divine reign on the throne with one of them at his right hand and one at his left hand, but he did not. Thomas thought he was an impostor who could not possibly rise from the dead, but he did. And so throughout all of history people have misunderstood him, just as his family misunderstood him.

Jesus could not entrust his mother's spiritual welfare to his family.

Today we still misunderstand Jesus. We want to make him into the kind of master that we want him to be, more like a servant who provides for us whatever it is that we want in life, instead of letting him make us into the kind of people he wants us to be. Only through obedience, love, and commitment can we ever understand Jesus and see him for what he really is.

That's exactly why Jesus commended his mother to John, because John's way of life was the way of obedience, love, and commitment. Jesus understood the importance of the spiritual well-being of his mother and knew that John was best fitted to help her. When Jesus commended his mother to John, it was more than an act of compassion and concern for her physical welfare, it was also concern for her spiritual well-being. He wanted her to be embraced by the warm fellowship of loyal, believing hearts.

> *"Why were there no males at the cross except John?"*

There is something infinitely moving in the fact that Jesus, in the agony of the cross, thought of the loneliness of his mother and of her great need in the days ahead. He never forgot the duties that were his. He was Mary's eldest son and even in the moment of his greatest struggle there on the cross, he did not forget the simple things that were his responsibility. At the end of his life, hanging on the cross, Jesus was thinking more of the sorrows and the needs of his mother than he was of himself. He entrusted his mother to John because John lived the way of obedience, love, and commitment.

Why was Mary, the mother of Christ, at the cross in the first place? Why wasn't she at home? Why didn't some well-meaning friend of Mary's prevent her from going to Golgotha? Surely, she ought not to see her son in the throes of the cruelest execution in the history of our world. Surely, she ought to remember him as he was in the days gone by. Surely, she should have been spared the sight of her son's crucifixion.

Probably not one, but many of Mary's friends sought to keep her as far as possible from the sight of the Crucifixion, but she would not stay away. Her mind was made up, and nothing could sway her from the hill of Golgotha. Mary was at the cross that day for the same reason that any of us would have been at the cross—she was there because she loved her son. That was the only place that Mary could have been. The scripture describes the scene: "standing near the cross of Jesus [was] his mother" (John 19:25*b*); a wonderful testimony to the love that was in Mary's heart.

With Mary at Golgotha were three other women: her sister, Salome, the mother of the beloved disciple John; Mary, the wife of Clopas; and Mary Magdalene. With the exception of John, there apparently was not another male disciple near the cross. Why were there no males at the cross except John? Robert J. McCracken writes that one Bible commentator, accounting for the presence of Mary and the other three women at Golgotha, and indirectly accounting for the absence of all the disciples except for John, said, "It was politically safe for the women to be there; no one ever bothered about women." Surely this is an inadequate and totally unacceptable explanation! Political consideration or no political consideration, danger or no danger, it would have been impossible to have kept Mary and those other three women from the cross.

Peter might deny him, Philip and James and Andrew might be afraid for their lives, Bartholomew might be hiding out nearby to watch. But what about the women? What did the jeering multitude mean to the women? Nothing! What fear did they have of the Roman soldiers? None! What peril was there for them from the might of the Roman Empire? None that they feared! For theirs was a love loyal unto death, even a death as gruesome as crucifixion. "Standing near the cross of Jesus [was] his mother" (John 19:25*b*). Human love is simply a reflection of divine love. The writer of the First Letter of John tells us: "We love because he first loved us" (1 John 4:19).

The story is told about a childless couple who wanted to adopt a little boy approximately six years old. They had visited several adoption agencies and finally found a child that was a match for their family. As they visited with the child the wife said, "If you would come and live with us you could have your own private room, a nice yard with play equipment and all the toys and clothes you could ever want. Would you like to come and live with us?" The little boy hesitated a moment and said, "No, I don't think so." The couple was stunned. They felt that they had offered the child everything a child could want. The husband said to the boy, "We've offered you everything anyone could want. What more do you want?" In words far beyond his years the child replied, "I just want someone to love me."

I expect that there are far more people today who are in distress because of a lack of love than there are people in distress for a lack of things. Mary was at the cross because Mary loved Jesus. "Standing near the cross of Jesus [was] his mother" (John 19:25*b*).

It was probably easy enough for Mary to love Jesus when he was little because a baby is very easy to love. Many mothers have said that the most joyous moments of their entire motherhood came in those early days when the child was totally dependent on them and just wanted the nourishment and love of the parent. As Jesus grew, there must have been occasions when his development eluded his mother and she did not understand what was happening. Many times she must have misunderstood what he was doing and saying, and there must have been times when his plans and dreams were beyond her comprehension.

When Jesus was twelve years old, his family went to Jerusalem for the feast of the Passover. When the festival ended and the family returned home, Jesus stayed behind in Jerusalem, but his parents did not know it. Assuming that he was in a group of travelers in a caravan, they went a day's journey. That night, they began to look for Jesus but could not find him. The next day they returned to Jerusalem and spent three days looking for him among their relatives and friends. They finally found him in the Temple, sitting among the teachers, listening to them and asking questions. What a strange place for Jesus to be at the age of twelve! "When his parents saw him, they were astonished; and his mother said to him, 'Child, why have you treated us like this? Look, your father and I have been searching for you in great anxiety.' He said to them, 'Why were you searching for me? Did you not know that I must be in my Father's house?'" (Luke 2:48-49). And the scripture said, "But they did not understand what he said to them" (Luke 2:50).

> "Mary never used her love to get her own way."

In spite of her lack of understanding on this and obviously other occasions in the time of the development of Jesus, Mary loved him with a real self-giving and unconditional love. She did not seek to control the direction of his life or make him into what she wished him to become. As far as we can tell, she never pleaded her love for him as a reason for his doing her will or repudiated him when he followed the path that he felt God had for him. Mary's love was a love that allowed Jesus to be what God had called him to be and that kind of love is true love. Self-possessive love only causes an emotional cripple. Mary never used her love to get her own way. Mary expressed the self-giving and unconditional love from the moment Jesus could understand and respond.

If we wish to express this kind of self-giving and unconditional love, we must learn that it is not a subject to be taught, it is a spirit to be caught. If we want to teach our children about love, we do not need to lecture them about love; we need to show them a self-giving and unconditional love that they might respond in the same way. If we wish to train our children in the appreciation of great literature, we do not need to give them a lecture about William Shakespeare and Elizabeth Barrett Browning; we need to expose them to the great passages of literature and let them find that appreciation for themselves. If we wish to teach our children to appreciate great music, we do not tell them what a great person Bach or Beethoven or Brahms was; we need to expose them to great music and let them discover for themselves the love of music. If we wish to teach our children about the great works of art, we do not give them lectures about art appreciation; we expose them to Van Gogh and Rembrandt, and let them experience the joy and beauty of great art.

The same is true in the development of the spiritual life of children. If we want a child to develop spiritually, we do not lecture to them about religion; we show them, by precept and example, what it is that we want them to learn. We do not tell them how helpful it would be if they read the Bible; we share the scripture with them in our homes, our churches, and our Sunday schools. We don't tell them that they need to learn to pray; we pray with them and teach them to pray, as we pray together as a family.

In my early childhood, my mother read a Bible story to me each night at bedtime. She did not tell me I ought to read the Bible; she shared a Bible story with me every night. She set an example for me to read the Bible. I grew up with the rich heritage of the Bible. That is a wonderful memory for me.

My parents always took me to church. They did not say, "It's wonderful if you go to church," or "You ought to go to church when you grow up," or "When you get old enough to decide, you ought to go to church." I grew up in a home where we went to church Sunday morning, Sunday night, and Wednesday night. I learned about church and religious values not because someone told me about them, but because somebody cared enough about me to see that they shared those values with me.

Mary's love for Jesus must have been something like that, the love of a mother for a child. Mary's love might well be summed up in Rudyard Kipling's poem, "Mother o' Mine."

> If I were hanged on the highest hill,
> *Mother o' mine, O mother o' mine!*
> I know whose love would follow me still,
> *Mother o' mine, O mother o' mine!*
> If I were drowned in the deepest sea,
> *Mother o' mine, O mother o' mine!*
> I know whose tears would come down to me,
> *Mother o' mine, O mother o' mine!*
> If I were damned of body and soul,
> I know whose prayers would make me whole,
> *Mother o' mine, O mother o' mine!*

"Standing near the cross of Jesus [was] his mother."

Fourth Word

From noon on, darkness came over the whole land until three in the afternoon. And about three o'clock Jesus cried with a loud voice, "Eli, Eli, lema sabachthani?" that is, "My God, my God, why have you forsaken me?"
(Matt. 27:45, 46)

"My God, my God, why have you forsaken me?"

The contempt, ridicule, and derision of the crowd had died away. The taunts, jeers, and insults of the soldiers had ceased. About noon the day had become as dark as night. For three long hours an unsettling darkness covered the hill of Golgotha. There was a strange uneasiness among those persons who lingered at the site of the Crucifixion. Apart from the centurion and the Roman guard, very few people remained.

Suddenly it seemed to the centurion that the great darkness was beginning to lift. He looked again at the man on the center cross, whose eyes were opened and whose face was lifted heavenward. He looked at the face of the man whose head was still crowned with those wicked spikes of thorns. He saw the dry, cracked lips move slowly and with much pain, and then there was a great cry: "Eli, Eli, lema sabachthani?" "Listen," some of the onlookers cried, "he is calling for Elijah!" But those who loved Jesus knew the meaning of his cry. It was part of a psalm that they had all known since childhood, and it meant, "My God, my God, why have you forsaken me?" (Matt. 27:46).

Why did Jesus feel that God had forsaken him? There was something very human in that cry to God. Jesus would not be the Savior of fallen humanity unless he had experienced the depths of human sorrow and despair. For him to have avoided or escaped the pain, sorrow, anguish, and suffering that is so much a part of human experience would have made him less real to us. Jesus suffered. He had sorrow and anguish and pain that were just as much a part of his human experience as they are a part of our human experience. Because of this we know that we do not have to experience what he has not already experienced.

> "There was nothing of the actor about
> Jesus."

His pain was as real as our pain. His cry of anguish was as real as our cry of anguish. His cry to God was a part of his experience of human suffering. As our life unfolds and as adversity enters into it, there are times when we feel that God has forsaken us. There are times when we come face to face with a situation beyond our comprehension and we feel that God has forgotten us. We have prayed for a loved one to live, but that loved one died. We have prayed that an illness might be cured, but that illness was not cured. We have prayed that there might be a positive resolution to conflicts and difficulties in our lives, but there was none. And in those moments we have cried out, "My God, my God, why have you forsaken me?" We can understand Jesus as he spoke in the midst of anguish and sorrow and suffering on the cross, and we empathize with him. We see Jesus in the midst of the ultimate human despair, suffering death on a cross, so that he can sympathize with our weaknesses. "My God, my God, why have you forsaken me?" is a familiar cry in our experience.

There was nothing of the actor about Jesus. He was always perfectly sincere and honest. He was not pretending to be in agony on the cross, he was not pretending to be something he was not. If Jesus was only fighting a sham battle, then it would have no meaning for us because our battles are real. We face pain, and we bear anguish and suffering and sorrow. If Jesus had not faced these same things, then he would not be able to empathize with our human condition.

> *"No person misses the presence of God more than one who has been keenly conscious of that presence."*

Jesus was speaking out of a sense of desolation. He felt that God had forsaken him in that terrible moment of agony. Part of that desolation came because of his physical torture. Jesus suffered upon the cross just as any human being would suffer if nailed to a cross. He endured four mock trials, he had been beaten with a whip, he had a crown of thorns placed upon his head that pierced his skin and caused blood to flow down upon his face, and he was forced to carry his cross on the road to Golgotha until he could carry it no longer. He had been on the cross for almost six hours in terrible, excruciating pain. It is not surprising that in the midst of his physical suffering Jesus cried out, "My God, my God, why have you forsaken me?"

Obviously, Jesus felt that his abandonment was utter and complete. He had been forsaken before this hour by the religious leaders among his own people; he had been forsaken by his family; he had been forsaken by his friends; he had been forsaken by his disciples—but he had not expected to come to the place where he felt that God had forsaken him.

No person misses the presence of God more than one who has been keenly conscious of that presence through the years. God had always been so real and so near to Jesus, but now he could not see his Father's face. His heartache was so much more painful when contrasted with the comfort that he had known. We often feel forsaken in the midst of our struggles. People throughout the ages can identify with the experience of feeling forsaken and alone in their suffering.

Centuries ago there lived a man named Job. He was rich in lands, his harvests were abundant, his barns bulged with crops and grains, his family setting was happy, his cattle multiplied, his wealth increased, and his reputation grew. In the vernacular of our day: "He had it made." He had everything that anyone could want. Suddenly, without warning, his whole world tumbled in upon him. He was stripped of his wealth, his harvests were destroyed, his family disintegrated, his barns were burned, his cattle were stolen, his wealth vanished, his sons died in a drunken brawl, his reputation withered, and he was smitten with a dire disease. What seems so unreasonable was that this came about through no perceived fault or transgression on Job's part. But nevertheless, his world tumbled in. Out of the dim and muffled past came this cry of Job, "But when I looked for good, evil came; and when I waited for light, darkness came" (Job 30:26).

This is part of the human dilemma. When something bad happens to us we say, "Why has this happened to me?

Why does God hide his face from me? Why has God forsaken me in the moment when I need God most?" The age-old story of Job is not really so old. It is relived and repeated thousands of times in every generation and culture. Job is not so much a personality as he is a representative of people; he is not so much an individual as a type of all humanity. Behind the heartbreaks that embitter, the sorrows that are never assuaged, the tears that do not dry, and the loneliness that is never healed, is the cry, "My God, my God, why have you forsaken me?" It is a part of our humanness. It was part of the humanness of Jesus. When we remember his anguish and pain and suffering, we remember that we do not have to experience what Jesus has not already experienced.

> *"We need to take the kingdom view and not judge God's whole plan by present events."*

Cancer strikes, a plane crashes, a foot slips on a ladder, a father suffers a heart attack, an automobile skids into a light pole, a mother dies and leaves a young family, a child is killed by a drunken driver, a breadwinner is laid off the job—and the all-too-human cry comes, "My God, my God, why have you forsaken me?"

"We know," said the apostle Paul, "that all things work together for good for those who love God, who are called according to his purpose" (Rom. 8:28). This does not mean that no unfortunate circumstance will ever come to us because we call ourselves Christians, or that no adversity will befall us because we belong to the church, or that all things will miraculously work out to our advantage because we are good people. No, that would be an unusual kind of love for God to bestow upon us, though most of us would like it. Just as steel is tempered in the fire, so also our lives are shaped by how we deal with the unalterable circumstances that come to us, undesired and unexpected.

We need to take the long view, to move beyond the present trials and tribulations of life, and to evaluate the present against the future. We need to take the kingdom view and not judge God's whole plan by present events. This is what the New Testament means when it teaches us to bear our present difficulties with steadfast endurance, to stand fast in the face of adversity, to keep the faith in moments of despair, knowing that all the events of life are part of the creative purpose of a loving God.

Most of us know how only a few short years can change our understanding of an event or circumstance in our lives. Something happened to us that seemed, at that moment, to be a great tragedy in our lives, and likely it was. We were resentful, we tried hard to avoid it, we did all we could to change it, and we cried out in bewilderment, "My God, my God, why have you forsaken me?" Yet how many times, as we look back upon that event or circumstance, has it turned out to be a turning point in our lives. It does not always happen this way, but when we love God and trust in God's way, we can trust the love of God in each circumstance of life.

Several weeks ago there appeared in the newspaper an article about a thirty-two-year-old man who stopped to help persons injured in an accident on a major city freeway. Another automobile crashed into the automobiles in the accident and threw the man who had stopped to help into the path of an oncoming automobile. The man was seriously injured and has spent months recovering. He has a wife, two small children, and mounting medical bills. In the interview for the article the writer asked the man if he would stop and help again in a similar situation. The man replied, "Certainly." He told the writer that he had thought time and again about the accident and often had asked, "Why me?" And then he said, "I thought one day, 'why not me?'"

> *"What most of us need in our adversity is not to find an explanation—but to find a victory."*

We do not know how this man's life will turn out or what the future holds for him, but one thing we know—his life will never be the same. That accident was a terrible event in his life. That does not mean his life will be worse for the event; it may be better. This is hard for us to understand and hard for us to accept. When things happen to us that we perceive as bad, these things bring a whole new perspective to life: sometimes they harden and embitter us; sometimes they toughen and strengthen us.

In different lives similar adversities produce strikingly different effects. One man loses his wife, and the loss makes him far more tender and gentle; another man faces the same loss, and it makes him hard and bitter. One woman faces a great sorrow, and it turns her to God; another woman faces a similar sorrow, and it turns her away from God.

What most of us need in our adversity is not to find an explanation—but to find a victory; it is not to elaborate a theory—but to lay hold upon a power. Even if the best and most completely satisfying answer to our question "why?" was available, that would not alter the fact that the actual suffering would still have to be endured.

There is a deeper question than "why?"—namely, "how?" The ultimate question is not "Why has this happened to

me?" but "How am I to face it?" When we see this, suddenly the New Testament begins to speak to us with a fresh
voice. The New Testament does not offer us a theory or an
explanation—it offers us a power and a victory. That is the
real demand of the human spirit—not an explanation of
what has happened, but the grace to help us bear it. And
that is why God gave us Christ. We do not have to experience what he has not already experienced.

"Was Jesus really forsaken?"

I was a very close friend to a family whose son was an
outstanding high school athlete. He was all-state running
back in his junior year in high school and was certain to be
a top choice of any university in the country when he grad-
uated from high school. The first game of his senior year
he suffered a back injury. The medical doctors told him
that if he had a similar injury to his back, it would in all
likelihood paralyze him for life. Obviously, playing football
became a thing of the past for him.

After his first semester in college he came home at the
Christmas break. Returning home about midnight from a
date, his automobile collided with an ambulance and he
was killed instantly. A brilliant young man was dead and a
lovely family devastated. Do we not understand the
anguished cry of the parents, "My God, my God, why have
you forsaken me?" As we hear Jesus' cry upon the cross, in
the midst of his own anguish and sorrow and suffering and
pain, we see the humanness of Jesus, and we know that we
do not have to experience what he has not already experienced.

Was Jesus really forsaken? We know that the answer is a
resounding "no." He was not forsaken. God was never as

close to his beloved Son as he was during those dark hours on the cross. We find assurance that God did not forsake Jesus in the knowledge that God never forsakes anyone. Often we forsake God, but God never forsakes us. When one sheep left the flock and strayed into the wilderness, the shepherd could not let that one sheep go. He went out and looked for the sheep until he found it and brought it home. And Jesus said, "God is like that." God is like the shepherd looking for the one lost sheep. He can never stop searching until he finds us. He never forsakes us however far we may go from him and however much we may rebel against him. Every promise that the saints of the centuries have shared with us assures us that God will never forsake those who trust him.

The one characteristic of God that is known by people of all faiths and all ages is God's faithfulness. They declare with one voice that God will never forsake us. The writer of the Letter to the Hebrews wrote, "For he has said, 'I will never leave you or forsake you'" (Heb. 13:5b). When Joshua was about to lead the children of Israel into the Promised Land, God said to him, "I will not fail you or forsake you. . . . Be strong and courageous; do not be frightened or dismayed, for the LORD your God is with you wherever you go" (Josh. 1:5b, 9). And in the book of Isaiah, God said to Israel, "Do not fear, for I am with you, do not be afraid, for I am your God; I will strengthen you, I will help you, I will uphold you with my victorious right hand" (Isa. 41:10).

> *"The cross of Christ is our strength."*

The biblical writers, the saints, and the church fathers declare with one voice, "God will not forsake us and God will not fail us." We, too, may face disappointment, anxiety, and pain, with the knowledge that God will not forsake us. When we feel anxious, forsaken, and full of fear about who we are and why we are here and where we are going and what we are going to do, the cross of Christ is our strength. When we are suffering pain and loneliness and heartache, we remember, "God will never leave us or forsake us." When we are angry and feeling guilty, the cross of Christ enables us to say with the psalmist, "God is our refuge and strength, a very present help in trouble" (Ps. 46:1).

Many years ago there was a young, active couple in the church. They were vibrant, loving, caring, and enthusiastic. They were deeply involved in the life of the church and the church was where they found their close friends. One day they announced that they were going to have their first child. There was excitement among the church members because they knew that this couple had wanted a child for several years. The months went by and a lovely little girl came to bless that home. There was joy and fullness of heart in the lives of the parents.

When the baby was a few months old she became very ill. She was rushed to the hospital and lived only a few hours. The death of that little child opened the hearts of the whole congregation. Out of the love of the people in their church during that most trying time, a whole new world of love, compassion, concern, and caring was opened to that young couple. Where they had previously been caregivers, they now became the recipients of the love and care of the members of their church family. Some days after the funeral they wrote to the people in their church.

Dear friends, our lovely daughter brought us nine months of excitement and anticipation before her coming and a lifetime of joy in her coming. And now the hurt of not being able to hold her close to us seems almost unbearable. When she died, something in us died too. We felt that God had forsaken us.

But because you prayed for us and because you love us, we will be able to move on with our lives. There is now a warm, living presence of the Risen Christ in our lives. He has given us a wonderful sense of God's peace. Along with his peace has come a new power and the realization that God will never forsake us. Keep on praying for us and keep on loving us. God does not forsake us. God does not fail us. Thanks be to God!

It was in that spirit that the young couple found peace and courage and strength through God to pick up the broken pieces of their lives and move forward. God does not forsake us! God does not fail us! We do not have to experience what Jesus has not already experienced.

Fifth Word

After this, when Jesus knew that all was now finished, he said (in order to fulfill the scripture), "I am thirsty."
(John 19:28)

"I am thirsty."

Jesus had been nailed to the cross for at least six hours. Pain and agony were his constant companions. His hands and feet were pierced deeply by rough, jagged nails. Each time he moved there was excruciating pain from the pull of the nails on his flesh. His head was still crowned with wicked spikes of thorns. Each movement of his head caused the thorns to pierce deeper. His back was striped with dried blood from the floggings. Each time he tried to become more comfortable on the cross he only opened up the wounds. The Romans had many methods of execution in Jesus' time, but crucifixion was the cruelest, the most horrible, and the most degrading of all. Crucifixion slowly destroyed the body, but the mind and spirit were not affected.

After having been in constant pain for hours, it is understandable that Jesus would say, "I am thirsty." Perhaps the real question is not, "Why did Jesus say these words?" but "Why did John record them in his Gospel?" It is my belief that he recorded them to show the humanity of Jesus. These words bring us face to face with the human qualities of Jesus. They bring us face to face with his human suffering. The words, "I am thirsty," reveal that when Jesus was on the cross he knew the human agony of thirst.

In order to understand why John would want to stress the humanness of Jesus we need to understand what was happening in the early Christian church at the time that John was writing. John wrote his Gospel around A.D. 100. At that period in the history of the early Christian church there had arisen a dangerous perversion of Christianity called Gnosticism. Its name comes from the Greek word for "knowledge" or "wisdom."

Out of Gnosticism came a movement called Docetism, which taught that spirit was good and matter was evil. Therefore, from their point of view, the body, which was matter, was totally evil. They concluded that God, who was pure spirit, could never have taken the form of a human body because the human body was evil. Therefore, they denied that Jesus had a real or natural body while on earth. They believed that Jesus had only an apparent or phantom body. They believed that when Jesus walked, his feet left no prints on the ground, because he was a pure spirit in a phantom body.

> "God was not playing games with us when Christ came."

The Docetists also believed that he could feel no real hunger or thirst; that he could feel no real pain or suffering; and that he could feel no real sorrow or sadness. They thought that he was a disembodied spirit in the apparent form of a man. They believed that God could never really suffer and therefore Jesus never really suffered on the cross.

The Docetists thought they were honoring God by denying that Jesus was able to suffer pain or die on the cross, but in reality, they were destroying Christ. From the point of view of the Gnostics, any real incarnation would be impossible, as would any real crucifixion, any real resurrection, or any real ascension. They concluded that God could not come in the human form of Christ. That is why John stressed the humanness of Jesus in his Gospel. That is why he stressed that Jesus felt thirsty. He wished to show that Jesus was really human, that he really suffered pain upon the cross, and that he really understood the agony of suffering. John stressed the real humanity and the real suffering of Jesus throughout his Gospel.

Jesus said, "I am thirsty." These words are the simple assurance today that God in Christ fully entered into the human situation, that he truly suffered, that there was pain and sorrow in his heart, and that he faced disappointment. God was not playing games with us when Christ came. Jesus had not placed a make-believe mask upon his face to pretend that he was human. Christ was God fully entering into the human condition and paying the price of experiencing human weakness and temptation.

The apostle Paul also understood the humanness of Jesus when he said, "that is, in Christ God was reconciling the world to himself" (2 Cor. 5:19). And to the early Christians at Philippi he taught:

> Let the same mind be in you that was in Christ Jesus,
> who, though he was in the form of God,
>> did not regard equality with God
>> as something to be exploited,
> but emptied himself,
>> taking the form of a slave,
>> being born in human likeness.
> And being found in human form,
>> he humbled himself
>> and became obedient to the point of death—
>> even death on a cross.   (Phil. 2:5-8)

53

John stressed the humanness of Christ in the Incarnation: God coming into the world in Christ. Jesus said, "I am thirsty." These three words assure us that he is one of us. He fully entered into the human situation. He comes to us as no stranger, but as one known among us, linked to us by the inseparable bonds of both body and spirit.

God was not like some well-meaning person who scheduled a brief visit through the poor section of town in order to distribute clothing and food, only to return to his or her nice home in the better section of town. No, God came into the world in Christ and made his home among the poor in order to endure what they had to endure—not enough food, inadequate clothing, prevalent crime, and the daily humiliations that the poor have to live with every single day. If God is ever to redeem us, God must become as we are, to make us what he is. This is the sign and seal of a genuine incarnation.

> "God had to become what we are in order to make us what God is."

This Christ whom we worship today as Lord and Savior is not some phantom who leaves no footprints on the ground as he walks, but he is God made human. He is the clearest revelation of God the world has ever known, yet at the same time he is the clearest revelation of what we are meant to be. The early church spoke of Christ as "very God, very man." God had to become what we are in order to make us what God is. Anything less would not have been God's way.

If Jesus were not fully human; if he had not suffered pain even as we suffer pain; if he had not become weary even as we become weary; if he had not had sorrow in his life even as we have sorrow; then, we could not identify with him. We would say he does not understand us. But God came in Christ to reconcile the world to himself so that we might identify with him, and that we might know that what we experience he has already experienced. He has walked the steps of pain, he has walked the paths of sorrow, he has hung upon the cross of pain, he has endured all that we ever will have to endure. There is no place we need to go where he has not been before.

Jesus said, "I am thirsty." The Christian faith teaches us that Jesus was fully human. Many earnest Christians feel that they cannot emphasize the humanity of Jesus without subtracting from his divinity. This is simply not true. If Jesus were not fully human, if his humanity were only a fabrication, then we would have no doctrine of revelation, we would have no doctrine of redemption, and we would have no Incarnation. God was fully human in the person of Christ.

We are often so eager to emphasize the fact that Jesus was fully God that we tend to forget that he was also fully human. We are often so eager to emphasize his divinity that we tend to forget his humanity. Christianity has proclaimed the divinity of Christ with the clarion call of a trumpet, but let there be no misunderstanding that it has also clearly sounded the conviction that he was vigorously and fully human. The First Letter of John was written at approximately the same period in history as the Gospel of John. The Gnostic heresy was at its height. John cautions the early Christians: "By this you know the Spirit of God: every spirit that confesses that Jesus Christ has come *in the flesh* is from God" (1 John 4:2, italics added). The first great theological battles waged by the Christian church were not to protect the idea of Christ's divinity against the claim that he was human; rather, they were fought to defend the fact of his humanity against the idea that he was only divine.

> *"Christ was no phantom figure too divine to suffer."*

In the face of heresies, Gnostic secrets, and various unsound doctrines active among the early churches, there was a need for the early Christians to clarify their own orthodox convictions. The best summary of early Christian beliefs is what we call today the Apostles' Creed. It is grossly inaccurate to believe that the apostles or the children of the apostles sat down and formulated a creed to frame their beliefs. It grew out of a need. It is only a sketchy outline of our faith. Scholars call the early version of it the Old Roman Guard. The Apostles' Creed is not so much a comprehensive statement of what we believe, as it is a rebuttal of the Gnostic heresy. The creed goes to great lengths to assert some essential human qualities that identify Christ with us in our humanness. The Apostles' Creed states that Jesus was: "born of the Virgin Mary, suffered under Pontius Pilate, was crucified, dead, and buried." All these are human experiences that identify him with us, disproving the belief that he was a phantom spirit living in a phantom body.

Ignatius, one of the early church fathers, was imprisoned and faced execution for his faith. He wrote to a group of churches in Asia Minor:

> Be deaf, therefore, when anyone speaks to you apart from Jesus Christ, who was of the family of David and Mary, who was truly born, both ate and drank, was truly persecuted under Pontius Pilate, was truly crucified and died. . . . But if as

some affirm, who are without God—that is, who are unbeliev-
ers—if suffering was only a semblance, why am I a prisoner?
                          (Ignatius, to the Trallians, 9, 10)

To the early Christian, Christ was no phantom figure too
divine to suffer. Our Christian faith has taught us from the
beginning that he was intensely human, sharing with us
the common human experiences of pain, suffering, and
sorrow, assuring us that what we experience he has already
experienced, and promising us that God is with us in every
event of life. There is no place we need to go where Christ
has not been before.

Throughout history, Christians have seen Christ's coming as a human event. His character is a human revelation
of what we might become. When we are depressed by pain,
suffering, and sorrow, he saves us from despair. Why?
Because he has been there before. He does not excuse us
when we believe that human nature, being what it is, causes us to be the way we are. Why? Because he has been that
way before. He knows there is something better for each of
us and his character has shown us that way. He gives sub-
stance to the hope that in all the limitations of our humanness we are yet meant for better things.

> *"There is no place we need to go where*
> *Christ has not been before."*

In the words of his Gospel, John tells us, "And the Word
became flesh and lived among us, and we have seen his
glory, the glory as of a father's only son, full of grace and
truth. . . . No one has ever seen God. It is God the only
Son, who is close to the Father's heart, who has made

him known" (John 1:14, 18). Perhaps nowhere else in the New Testament do we see the humanity of Jesus so fully proclaimed. In Jesus we see God living life as he would have lived it if he had been a human being. If we said nothing else about Jesus, we could still say that he shows us how God would live life day by day. He identifies with us, we identify with him, and we know that there is no place we need to go where he has not been before.

When John was writing his Gospel, it was extremely important to show the humanity of Jesus in order that persons might identify with that humanity. When Jesus cries, "I am thirsty," that humanity is revealed to its fullest. Those three words tell us that what we experience he has already experienced.

Here we meet the Risen Christ. He is near to us in our humanity to lead the way to what, under God, we might become. He is above us in his divinity to release powers in us greater than our own, through which we become what we could not become without him. He is with us even in pain and sorrow and suffering, to bring through them God's perfect will in our lives. There is no place we need to go where he has not been before.

> "The road is rough, dear Lord," I said,
>   "There are stones that hurt me so."
> "Yes, child," He answered, "I understand
>   For I walked it long ago."
>
> "But there is a cool green path," I said,
>   "Let me walk in it for a time."
> "No, child," He answered,
>   "The green path doesn't climb."
>
> "My burden Lord is far too great,
>   How can I bear it so."

I Am Thirsty

"Yes, child, I remember its weight,
   For I carried my cross you know."

"But I wish there were friends with me,
   who would make my way their own."
"Yes, child," He answered, "Gethsemane
   Was hard to face alone."

And then I picked my burden up,
   Content at last to know,
That where he had not been
   I would not need to go.

And strangely then, I found new friends,
   My burden seemed less sore,
When I remembered long ago,
   He went that way before!

Author Unknown

Sixth Word

> *A jar full of sour wine was standing there. So they put a sponge full of the wine on a branch of hyssop and held it to his mouth. When Jesus had received the wine, he said, "It is finished." Then he bowed his head and gave up his spirit.*
> *(John 19:29-30)*

"It is finished."

The eerie darkness had lifted, gradually daylight returned. The physical strength of Jesus was diminishing. He cried out, "My God, my God, why have you forsaken me?" After a period of silence came the very human cry, "I am thirsty." By this time most of the crowd at the cross had gone home. As the ominous darkness changed to bright afternoon light, Jesus said, "It is finished." What was finished? The work that God had sent Jesus to do was now finished with his death upon the cross, but not the work that God has for us to do.

Near death, Jesus proclaimed that his task was finished; he had completed the work that God had sent him to do. No one had a greater love for life than Jesus, no one had a deeper realization of what could be accomplished by living than he had. At the same time, no one had ever been given a greater work than he had been given. He had spent approximately three years trying to do what God had sent him to do. He sought to train his disciples to carry on his work so that there might be some kind of future for it after he was gone. But one of them had betrayed him, another had denied him, and all had fled at the first sign of danger. Jesus had barely begun the work when he had to quit. He said, "It is finished." What was finished? The work that God had sent him to do was finished with his death upon the cross, but not the work that God has for us to do.

The statement, "It is finished," is three words in English, but it is one word in Greek. As Jesus said it, it might be better translated "finished," or "completed," or "done." "It is finished" is the victor's shout: "It is finished! I have done what God asked me to do, I have accomplished that which he sent me to accomplish." The word *finished* described those who had completed their task, those who had survived the struggle, those who had come out of the dark into the glory of the light. It was the cry of those who had won the victory!

> "*The cross did not cancel out what Jesus had accomplished.*"

The victors are those who refuse to believe that God has forsaken them even when in every fiber of their being they feel that God has forsaken them. The victors are those who will never let go of their faith even when they feel that the foundation of their faith is gone. The victors are those who have been beaten by life but who still hold onto God. The cross did not cancel out what Jesus had accomplished. The cross stands today as the affirmation that God's love can never be thwarted, that even in apparent defeat the ultimate victory belongs to God. The apostle Paul reminds us that "in Christ God was reconciling the world to himself" (2 Cor. 5:19). Paul affirms that God was in Christ. God was in Christ in those last hours. God was in Christ in those last words. God was in Christ when he said, "It is finished."

What was the work Jesus had to do? Jesus came to preach the good news, to reveal God's love for God's people, to speak the truth in love, to inaugurate the kingdom of heaven, to reconcile people to God and to one another, to heal the sick, to bless the poor, to comfort those in sorrow. Jesus said in effect, "My work is finished. That which God asked me to do I have accomplished. It is finished." What was finished? The work that God had sent him to do was finished with his death upon the cross, but not the work that God has for us to do.

Jesus told his disciples a parable about those who continue to do his work and those who do not. It is often called "the parable of the great judgment." Jesus said that "when the Son of Man comes in his glory," he will separate people into two groups as a shepherd separates the sheep from the goats. Those who are favored will inherit the kingdom. But what will these chosen people have done to be so blessed?

> "I was hungry and you gave me food, I was thirsty and you gave me something to drink, I was a stranger and you welcomed me, I was naked and you gave me clothing, I was sick and you took care of me, I was in prison and you visited me." Then the righteous will answer him, "Lord, when was it that we saw you hungry and gave you food, or thirsty and gave you something to drink? And when was it that we saw you a stranger and welcomed you, or naked and gave you clothing? And when was it that we saw you sick or in prison and visited you?" And the king will answer them, "Truly I tell you, just as you did it to one of the least of these who are members of my family, you did it to me."
>
> (Matt. 25:35-40)

Are we able to grasp the significance of what Jesus was saying to his disciples and to us as his followers today? We are to carry on the mission that he started. How do we do this? We do this by simple, humble everyday actions of loving-kindness that anyone can do. It requires no special talent, no special skill, no special education, no special training. It requires only the ability to love and care about other people. That is something each of us can do.

There is a story in the Gospel of John about Jesus and the disciples gathering in the upper room on the night before the Crucifixion. They came for a meal together. There were no paved roads in Jesus' day and the open sandals people wore allowed their feet to become dusty and dirty as they walked the roads. According to the tradition of the times, the host would have a basin of water and a towel at the door and wash and dry the feet of the guests.

When the disciples were gathered in the upper room, they all wanted to be the most important and none wanted to wash the feet of another. They sat and looked at one another, none willing to be the servant. Hear the Gospel of John:

> And during supper Jesus, knowing that the Father had given all things into his hands, and that he had come from God and was going to God, got up from the table, took off his outer robe, and tied a towel around himself. Then he poured water into a basin and began to wash the disciples' feet and to wipe them with the towel that was tied around him.
>
> (John 13:2*b*-5)

Jesus took upon himself the role of a servant, who was willing to wash the feet of his disciples. Jesus, knowing that he was in a unique relationship with God, did that menial task out of love for others, and to set an example for his disciples, that they might show the same spirit of humility and love toward one another. This is the gospel in action.

Legend has it that near the end of his life the apostle John was carried into his church at Ephesus for a final word to his congregation. What would the beloved disciple of Jesus say to that congregation at the end of his life? "Beloved," he said, "let us love one another" (1 John 4:7*a*). Love for one another is an act of human compassion and concern that each of us can fulfill every day. It does not cost anything, it does not require anything special except the willingness to pour out our love one for another. Jesus said, "It is finished." What was finished? The work that God had sent him to do was finished with his death upon the cross, but not the work God has for us to do.

> *"We are not in the world for our own joy."*

A man had given his life to the ministry of the poor and disenfranchised in the slums of New York City. He was in poor health and often discouraged. He was asked by a friend, "Why don't you just run away from it all before you are broken by this inhuman burden that you have placed upon yourself?" The man replied, "I would like to run away from it all, but a strange man on the cross won't let me." "It is finished." What was finished? The work that God had sent him to do was finished with his death upon the cross, but not the work that God has for us to do.

We are not in the world for our own joy. We are not here for our own pleasure. We are not here for our own self-gratification. We are here because God has placed us in this world to be instruments of God's purpose and will for this world.

It is a wonderful thing to know that we are "right with God," that we are converted, that we are born again. But after awhile such experiences become stale and unsatisfying, unless we are practicing the good news of God's redeeming love in Jesus Christ by witnessing and by our sharing our faith with others; unless we are positively assisting the work of God's church; and unless we are definitely bringing to bear upon actual human situations the pattern of Christian living. In other words, unless we are acting out our beliefs day by day, unless we do what we say, unless we live as we believe, our proclamations become as "a noisy gong or a clanging cymbal."

What are some things we can do as individual Christians each day? We can visit the sick, the shut-ins, the homebound, and the lonely. Unless we have been sick or shut-in or homebound, we do not know how lonely life can be; we do not know how left out of life we can feel; we do not know how shut off from the rest of society we can become. What a wonderful and compassionate thing it is to say, "We care."

> *"The only way the church continues to exist is as we share our faith with others."*

Our church has a wonderful lay visitation ministry that is called "We Care" because that is what they do. They care! They care about our homebound and shut-in members who live alone or who are confined to a nursing home. Most of these persons were active members of our congregation for years, but for health reasons they cannot be active today. The ministry started with a few committed persons. One of our laypersons said, "I believe in that ministry. I believe it is what we ought to be doing as a part of our church." He volunteered to give himself full-time to that ministry. He has helped us to recruit almost three hundred people, who each take the responsibility for one homebound or shut-in person in our congregation. These homebound people need the tender love and care that another person can provide, the warmth and concern and genuineness of feeling one person can have for another.

We can do such a caring thing as delivering a warm meal to someone who might not ever have one. A ministry that takes warm meals out into the community each day to share with needy people communicates love and concern along with the food itself. An individual could do this once a week.

We can teach children. We can nurture youth. Most of us can remember someone who taught us in Sunday school or who shared their faith with us or who helped us to grow as young Christians. Perhaps it was a parent, a grandparent, a Sunday school teacher, a youth worker, a counselor, someone who lifted us up and helped us to understand the great truth of our faith. It has been said that the Christian church is always only one generation away from extinction. Anytime one generation decides that its faith is not worth passing on to someone else, the Christian church is just that much closer to extinction. The only way we continue to exist is as we share our faith with others.

We have church buildings in which we worship because people shared their faith and believed in the church enough to build buildings where future generations might worship. We have a Bible to read because people hundreds of years ago believed enough in their faith to write that faith down, to transmit it, to share it, and to pass it from generation to generation. People were burned at the stake because they were willing to translate the scripture into English so that the common people might read it.

We can serve as ushers or greeters. We can say to those who come to the church, "We are glad you came to worship with us today." We can help to prepare the communion elements used each Sunday in our worship services. We take so many things for granted, but someone has to come early every Sunday and prepare the communion elements for us.

We can serve in the many and varied ministries of our church all the way from West Dallas to Haiti. We can serve because we care. We can serve in the various ministries that our church sponsors all across our city, our nation, and our world because this is the work we have to do.

> "If the church is to be ablaze with the truth of God . . . we must be prepared to meet the cost."

The influence of the Christian fellowship upon children, upon youth, and upon the community would be vastly enhanced today if even half the existing members of our church were to give one single hour of dedicated service each week through their church. To do such a thing, just for one hour each week, is costly and a hundred different excuses crowd readily into our minds. But if the church is to be ablaze with the truth of God, and full of the warmth of God's love, we must be prepared to meet the cost and make the sacrifice.

Thomas à Kempis, a fifteenth-century monk, wrote what has become a religious classic, *The Imitation of Christ*. One section in that book reads:

> Jesus hath now many lovers of His heavenly kingdom, but few bearers of His Cross. Many He hath that are desirous of consolation, but few of tribulation. Many He findeth that share his table, but few His fasting. All desire to rejoice with Him, few are willing to endure any thing for Him. Many follow Jesus unto the breaking of bread; but few to the drinking of the Cup of His Passion. Many reverence His miracles, few follow the shame of His Cross.
>
> (Book II, chapter 11)

We have a wonderful couple in our church who have been very active members for many years and have given their service in many different areas. About two years ago, this couple was asked to join with a group of laypeople who would lead a daily Bible study at an inner city ministry. They were asked to teach one day a week. They minister primarily to homeless people, most of whom have no place to sleep, no jobs, very little money, and no place to call home. They are poor, they are underprivileged, they are disenfranchised.

This couple agreed, thinking that they were offering a service, not realizing that it would be one of the most blessed experiences of their life. Let me share with you what the man wrote about one of his experiences.

"One day we announced the morning Bible study and were waiting for the participants to gather before boarding the elevator for a second floor classroom. An older man, with a thoughtful look on his face, stood next to me. I said to him, 'Good morning, friend, how are you today?' 'Real fine,' the man replied, 'except for one thing. Would you pray for some socks for me? These socks I have on are really itching me bad and I just have to get some new socks before these drive me crazy.' 'Sure,' I said, 'I will pray for you.'

"And suddenly I thought, I have a whole drawer full of socks at home. Why don't I just give him the ones I have on? They're clean. I put them on fresh this morning. He might not have another chance to get a pair of socks soon. I sat down on the floor and proceeded to remove my shoes, take off my socks, and offer them to him. 'I'll answer your prayers right now,' I said. 'Here take my socks. They are clean. I put them on fresh this morning.' Reluctantly he took my socks and exchanged them for the ones he was wearing. I asked him how they felt. He thanked me profusely and exclaimed, 'My feet feel just like they are in heaven now.'

"I didn't think any more about it and we went on to our classroom. That morning we were studying the twenty-fifth chapter of Matthew concerning the great judgment. As we were discussing the section where the king was speaking to those at his right hand and assuring them of their place in the kingdom because they had responded by giving food when he was hungry, drink when he was thirsty, welcoming when he was a stranger, clothing him when he was naked, visiting him when he was sick, I was beginning to feel a little uneasy. Here we were trying to teach a lesson about caring for the needy to those who obviously were in great need. At the time it seemed it would be more appropriate to be teaching a lesson on hope and salvation to this group rather than service to others. How little did I understand!

> *"When we are unable to receive, we are denying someone the opportunity to give."*

"As the discussion progressed we came to the section where the righteous asked the king when they saw him in such a situation. As we came to the verse where the question is asked, 'When did we see you naked and clothe you?' a member of the group suddenly interrupted. 'I know what this means,' he said, 'because I saw it myself this morning when the preacher here (nodding toward me!) sat down and took off his socks and gave them to this other man who needed them.' Another member asked, 'Did you really give him your socks?' He reached into a ruffled old knapsack and took out a pair of socks neatly rolled into a tight little ball. 'Here,' he said, 'I have an extra pair. Take these, they're clean, put them on.' 'No, really,' I replied, 'I have plenty of socks at home,' knowing that the poor fellow was probably offering me his only other pair of socks and I didn't want to take something that he needed more than I did. But he was persistent in his offer. I was about to reject his offer a second time when a small voice deep inside me said, 'Bill, you don't understand. It is not that you need his socks, it's that he needs to give you his socks. If you are not willing to receive his gift then you will deny him the opportunity to give.' With great humility I received his socks and immediately put them on and he smiled at me. I believe this was the first time I ever realized how interwoven are the acts of giving and receiving. When we are unable to receive, we are denying someone the opportunity to give. That pair of socks is now my most cherished possession."

"Just as you did it to one of the least of these who are members of my family, you did it to me" (Matt. 25:40b). Friends, our work is not finished.

Seventh Word

It was now about noon, and darkness came over the whole land until three in the afternoon, while the sun's light failed; and the curtain of the temple was torn in two. Then Jesus, crying with a loud voice, said, "Father, into your hands I commend my spirit." Having said this, he breathed his last.
(Luke 23:44-46)

"Father, into your hands I commend my spirit."

The time of Jesus' death had come. He had cried, "It is finished." The centurion and the Roman guard remained. It was their job to see that the crucifixion of the prisoners was completed and that no one came to take them down from the crosses. The centurion remembered that the man on the center cross seemed to have had several friends present for the crucifixion. Perhaps they might try to rescue him, although by now he must be almost dead. Then the centurion remembered that those followers, if they might rightly be called that, had all fled like cowards when the prisoners were nailed to the crosses.

Suddenly there was a loud cry from the prisoner on the center cross, "Father, into your hands I commend my spirit." These last words that Jesus spoke from the cross come from Psalm 31, a psalm of great trust and confidence in God. Jesus added one word, *Father:* "Father, into your hands I commend my spirit." Jesus died with a Jewish prayer on his lips. That verse from Psalms was the first prayer that every Jewish mother taught her child to pray during evening prayers. Much as some of us were taught, "Now I lay me down to sleep," the Jewish mother taught her child to pray before the coming night, "Into your hands I commit my spirit." Even on the cross Jesus had an unfailing trust in the goodness of God.

These final words of Jesus are a proclamation of victory. They follow directly his words, "It is finished," another cry of victory. He was affirming that God leads us to triumph when all the circumstances of life seem against us. Nothing, not even the agony of the cross, changed Jesus' witness to the love and concern and victory of God. "Father, into your hands I commend my spirit." This prayer was an act of commitment—a proclamation of victory.

Dr. James Moffatt, one of our great biblical translators, gives this translation of those words: "Father, I trust my spirit to your hands." Jesus died as he lived, with a great trust and confidence in God, with a firm faith in the goodness of God, and with an unwavering commitment to God. Jesus prayed in the garden of Gethsemane, "Father, if you are willing, remove this cup from me; yet, not my will but yours be done" (Luke 22:42). He was concerned that God's will would be done. All of his life Jesus had committed himself to God, and at his death he had that same firm commitment.

H. R. McIntosh, commenting on Jesus' commitment, wrote: "The great reason we fail to understand Calvary is not merely that we are not profound enough; it is that we are not good enough. It is because we are such strangers to sacrifice that God's sacrifice leaves us bewildered." Jesus' sense of commitment was so firm throughout his life, that at the time of his death he could surrender himself to God and say, "Father, into your hands I commend my spirit."

These words sum up what both life and death meant to Jesus; they also sum up what life and death ought to mean to us. If we are willing to make this kind of commitment to God, if we are willing to trust our lives and our spirits to God, we may be certain that our commitment will enable us to stand firm, both in the midst of daily living and when we come to the end of life's journey, just as it did for Jesus.

"Neutrality is always surrounded by dangers."

Jesus told his disciples a parable in which he was obviously comparing an empty life to an empty house. In Jesus' day people believed in evil spirits. An evil spirit is expelled from a man's home. The man drives out the evil spirit, cleans his home thoroughly, and then considers the job complete. The evil spirit wanders through "waterless regions," seeking rest but finding none, and decides to return to what he calls "my house." He is overjoyed to find that it is "empty, swept, and put in order," for no better tenant has replaced him. He leaves and brings back seven other spirits, each more evil than himself, and they enter and live there. And, says Jesus, "the last state of that person is worse than the first" (see Matt. 12:43-45).

In this parable Jesus teaches a profound spiritual lesson. The empty mind, the empty heart, the empty life are like an empty house. The peril of neutrality lies just here: in its emptiness. It is neither for nor against. It is bland and lukewarm. It has no vitality. Neutrality is always surrounded by dangers. We must make a commitment to the One whom we shall serve or by default our lives will be filled with a hundred different masters.

> *"The condition of discipleship is this: Christ or nothing!"*

It is the mark of great leaders that they should clearly state the terms of their discipleship. Garibaldi, the Italian patriot said, "Soldiers, what I have to offer you is fatigue, danger, struggle, and death; the chill of the cold night in the free air, and heat under the burning sun; no lodgings, no munitions, no provisions, but forced marches, dangerous watch posts, and continual struggle with bayonets against batteries. Those who love freedom and their country may follow me."

But no leader ever required more than Jesus. Uncompromisingly he warned his followers against a halfhearted discipleship. He stated that the cost of following him was complete commitment of self to him and his way. Plainly stated, the condition of discipleship is this: Christ or nothing! He said, "If any want to become my followers, let them deny themselves and take up their cross and follow me" (Matt. 16:24).

Jerry Kramer was a twelve-year veteran of the National Football League, winning fame as a member of the Green Bay Packers in their great years. He played in the offensive line as a guard and probably was best known as a "pulling guard," one who moved from his position and went in front of the runner as a blocker. After he retired he wrote a book entitled *Instant Replay*. In his book he tells about playing under Coach Vince Lombardi, recognized as one of the greatest professional football coaches. The thing that impressed me the most about Kramer's book was the incredible price that professional athletes have to pay in terms of physical conditioning, mental discipline, and emotional agony.

Lombardi was a coach who demanded perfection from everyone in the organization—the players, the coaches, the trainers—even the equipment personnel. Kramer tells how different players reacted to that kind of strict regimentation. Every year, he said, there was a fresh crop of rookies, most of whom were not there at the end of training camp. Some quit because they couldn't take the discipline. Some quit because they didn't want to take the discipline. Some quit because they lacked the commitment to do the job. These players chose to drop out rather than endure the discipline.

It is a long way from the training camp of the Green Bay Packers to the banks of the River Jordan. But in another way it is not far at all. If a person wants to achieve in life— whatever his or her calling—there must be that sense of commitment. If we as Christians are to be true followers of Christ, we must be willing to commit our spirits into his hands.

Commitment is the willingness to trust our lives to God. How do we make this commitment? Our experiences are varied since we are all different. We do not all react in the same fashion. We do not do the same things in identical circumstances. But there are characteristics of commitment that are common to all of us: surrender of our will to God's will and obedience to follow God's will for our lives.

We enter the Christian life by the willingness to trust our lives to God because there is no other way. We enter the Christian life by the way of surrender and obedience because there is no other way. Jesus said, "Not my will but

75

yours be done" (Luke 22:42*b*). That is surrender. Jesus said, "My food is to do the will of him who sent me and to complete his work" (John 4:34). That is obedience. The way of surrender and obedience is hard for most of us, not because we *do not* understand what they mean, but because we *do* understand what they mean. We do not have the courage to act on them.

Look at the commitment of one of Jesus' disciples. The scripture relates that as Jesus was walking along he saw a man called Matthew sitting at the tax booth and he said to him, "Follow me." Do you remember what happened? Did Matthew tell Jesus he needed to go home and get his affairs in order? Did he tell Jesus he even needed to pray about it? Did he debate with Jesus? We do not know. We only know one thing. We are only told that he made a commitment to follow Jesus. The scripture says, "And he got up and followed him" (Matt. 9:9*b*). He made a commitment of himself then and there. Thus he entered the kingdom of believers and followers of Christ. That is the way we must walk—the way of commitment to God.

> *"Earthly things always seem so real; heavenly things always seem so imaginary."*

Jesus told another story about a rich young ruler seeking eternal life. He had everything going for him. He was a person of integrity, he was religious, he was courageous. Yet, when Jesus gave him the same invitation he gave to Matthew, "Come and follow me," the rich young ruler did not make the same response. Jesus knew the young man's heart. If he truly wanted to make a commitment to follow Jesus, he would have to count the cost. Jesus told him, "Go, sell what you own, and give the money to the poor, and then you will have treasure in heaven; then come, follow me" (Mark 10:21). Jesus offered the rich young man heavenly, permanent riches "where neither moth nor rust consumes" in exchange for earthly, perishable riches. That offer was refused. His response was this tragic word, "When he heard this, he was shocked and went away grieving, for he had many possessions" (Mark 10:22). His possessions seemed so real and tangible; the rewards of heaven seemed so intangible. Earthly things always seem so real; heavenly things always seem so imaginary.

He missed entering the kingdom, not because he was a bad person or because he did bad things or because he associated with bad persons. He missed entering the kingdom because he refused to make a commitment of himself to God. Jesus said, "Father, into your hands I commend my spirit." Jesus made that commitment to God.

William Booth was a Methodist minister in England. When he could not do the work he wanted to do within the confines of the institutional church, he did the work he wanted to do on his own. Out of that work came what we know today as the Salvation Army, one of the finest ministries for the underprivileged in the world. Asked for the secret of his success in the Salvation Army, Booth replied, "I will tell you the secret. God has had all of me there was. There have been men with greater brains than I, men with great opportunity. But the day I got the poor of London on my heart and caught a vision of what Jesus Christ could do for them, on that day I made up my mind that God should have all of William Booth there was. And if there is anything of power in the Salvation Army today, it is because God has had all of the adoration of my heart, all the power of my will, and all of the influence of my life." William Booth had that commitment to God. His life was lived in surrender and obedience. Without a doubt he said, "Father, I trust my spirit in your hands."

> "Without the ability to reject, the ability to accept means very little."

In the fifteenth chapter of Luke there are three stories, all of them having to do with a loss. A woman lost a coin. A shepherd lost a sheep. A father lost a boy. When the woman discovered that her coin was missing she went searching for it. When she found it she picked it up and put it back in its proper place. When the shepherd discovered one of his sheep was missing he went searching for it until he found it and he brought it back and put it in the fold. Did it ever occur to you that the father did not go searching after his son? I think the father knew where his son was. People did not travel far in that time in ancient Israel. Why didn't the father go and get the son and bring him back home and say to him, "Son, I'm going to take you home and you're going to be good whether you want to or not." The answer is: a forced commitment is not commitment, but control.

When God created us, he created us with a free will and with the ability to accept or reject what is offered to us. Without the ability to reject, the ability to accept means very little. If the father had brought his son home over the protests of his son, the son would have been as much a prodigal at home as he was in the far country. The turning point in the prodigal's life came when he reached the place where he said out of his own free will, "I will arise and go to my father." The only time commitment means anything to anyone is when we say, "I will arise and go to my father who is in heaven." The only time commitment means anything is when we are willing to say, "Father, into your hands I commend my spirit."

Polycarp was bishop of Smyrna in the second century A.D. He was eighty-six years old when the Romans dragged him into the arena and demanded that he renounce his faith. Polycarp chose to be burned at the stake rather than speak the few simple words that would save him. John Wycliffe translated the scriptures into English so that the common people could read them. He faced hatred, hardships, and misunderstanding because he wanted to spread the Word of God. Joan of Arc was burned at the stake because she acted under what she believed were the direct commands of God rather than those of the church.

> "To those who are called, the cross is the power of God and the wisdom of God."

St. Francis turned his back on a comfortable life and traveled the world preaching repentance and begging bread. Jane Addams gave up a life of luxury to found Hull House in the slums of Chicago. Muriel Lester gave up a promising career to start Kingsley Hall for women in London. The name Florence Nightingale conjures up all that is good and worthwhile in nursing. These people all had one thing in common—a commitment of their lives to God. Commitment is the willingness to trust our lives to God.

Louis Pasteur, French chemist and bacteriologist, discovered a method of preventing fermentation in milk, a process called pasteurization. What gave Louis Pasteur the power to do for France and the world what would make all people his debtors and his name immortal? One whole side of his body was completely paralyzed at the age of forty-three. He was taunted, ridiculed, and humiliated by the citizens of his town. When food was needed for the soldiers in the time of war, he was told that he was only another useless mouth to feed. But he went on to do something for France that men with guns have never been able to do. He revealed his secret when he said, "The secret of what I have been able to do is in the One I surrendered my life to—Christ made me what I am."

Commitment involves surrender of our will to God's will and obedience to follow God's will for our lives. To those who are called, the cross is the power of God and the wisdom of God. The denial of oneself for God's sake, the bearing of one's cross, the turning of the other cheek, the walking of the second mile, the bearing of another's burden, the loving of one's enemies—all these are the power and the wisdom of God, because we are willing to take up our cross for his sake and to follow him. And until we are willing to say, "I will arise and go to my Father," we are going to live the life of the prodigal, a life that promises to deliver wealth and happiness, but never does.

> *But on the first day of the week, at early dawn, they came to the tomb, taking the spices that they had prepared. They found the stone rolled away from the tomb, but when they went in, they did not find the body. While they were perplexed about this, suddenly two men in dazzling clothes stood beside them. The women were terrified and bowed their faces to the ground, but the men said to them, "Why do you look for the living among the dead? He is not here, but has risen."*
> *(Luke 24:1-5)*

"Easter proclaims good news."

H e is not here, but has risen." And we ask, "How can that be?" Last winter I walked around the church to see how the grounds looked. The grass had patches of brown. The leaves had fallen from many of the trees. There was one tree that was naked and barren. I thought, "That tree is dead. It will never make it through the winter." I snapped a branch from the tree and it cracked because it was so dry and brittle. I thought, "That is a tree we will have to replace in the spring."

But that tree made a remarkable recovery. In the spring there was new growth on the branches and the leaves filled out the tree. That seemingly dead tree had returned to life. How could that be? A tree that appeared to be dead was now alive.

As I was preparing this sermon for Easter Sunday I thought, "If that seemingly dead tree, naked and barren in the winter, can sprout new growth and beautiful new leaves in the spring, why do we find it so difficult to believe in life eternal through God? If God, in this vast universe has made so many wonderful things that come alive, though we think they are dead, why do we not believe that God has done the same thing for the greatest of all God's creations?"

This is the good news that Easter brings to us—the good news that he is not here, but has risen.

"Easter proclaims good news about God."

Easter proclaims that at the heart of the universe is not just something, but Someone. That Someone is God and God cares about us and God loves us. Easter proclaims good news about God. Easter proclaims that the world is not just a gigantic machine shop filled with machinery that rusts and wears out and is cast upon the scrap heap. Easter proclaims that the world is not just a whirling ball in space that is spinning around and going nowhere. Easter proclaims that the world is not just a stream of frustrating days and endless nights. No, Easter proclaims the good news of God's love. Easter proclaims the good news that God's love is the ultimate power in the universe and that God sent that love to us in Jesus Christ, crucified yet risen. He is here! He is risen, just as he said he would.

In Walter de la Mare's poem "The Listeners," the poet asks the ultimate question:

"Is there anybody there?" said the Traveller,
　　Knocking on the moonlit door;
And his horse in the silence champed the grasses
　　Of the forest's ferny floor.
　　　　　　　(Walter de la Mare, "The Listeners")

We are all travelers journeying through life, knocking on the door of the universe and asking, "Is anybody there?" And the Easter faith proclaims to us, "Yes, there is somebody there, and that somebody is God and God loves us and God cares about us." The God who loves us and cares about us causes the trees to blossom in the spring, the flowers to come into full bloom, the dead-looking grain of corn to sprout into a cornstalk with new ears of corn. And we say, "How can that be?" And the God who answers our knock upon the universe door says, "Because I love you and care about you."

Eternal life is believable because we believe somebody is there and that somebody is God. We believe that the God who created the human personality can and will preserve that personality. We do not believe that life ends with death. The chisel falls and the sculpture is incomplete. The artist's brush is laid down and the painting is unfinished. The writer lays down the pen and the book does not have a last chapter. The architect lays down the sketch pad and unfinished dreams are locked in the mind of that architect. Are we then to assume that all is lost? Are we to believe that that is all there is? Is everything now finished?

Perhaps Victor Hugo said it best. Near the close of a great life when he had accomplished so many things he wrote: "For half a century I have been putting my thoughts in prose and in verse. History, philosophy, drama, romance, tradition, satire, ode and song—I've tried them all. But, I feel I've not said yet a thousandth part of what is in me. When I go to the grave I can say like so many others, 'I have finished my life,' but I cannot say I have finished my work. My day's work will begin anew the next morning. My tomb is not a blind alley, it is a thoroughfare. It closes in the twilight only to open to the dawn."

It is difficult for me to believe that God, who has created us with a yearning for immortality, a longing for that which is not yet finished, would betray us in the fulfillment of that immortality. Someone has said that the strongest argument for immortality is not the nature of people, but the character of God. Easter proclaims the good news about God, a God who loves us and cares about us.

> *"Easter proclaims good news about people."*

"Where does your great river go?" David Livingston would frequently ask the natives of the interior of Africa, pointing to the Congo River. "It is lost in the sand," the natives would always reply for they had never seen the sea to which the river surely and swiftly would go.

"If a person dies, shall he live again?" we frequently ask ourselves. And in moods of discouragement and fatigue we answer, "How can it be?" Because we cannot see the distant sea, we assume, with the natives of Africa, that the sea does not exist. Because our finite minds cannot comprehend the eternal nature of God's love, we assume that our lives at death are lost in the sands of time. But Easter says this is not true. The Easter message of victory over death brings to our ears the roar of the distant sea that we cannot see, but know is there. Easter is good news about people because it is good news about God's love and forgiveness; it is good news about God's victory over death in the resurrection of Christ.

To a great many persons the resurrection story sounds incredible. "People do not rise from the grave," they say, "how can this be?" But people have observed that all progress prior to experience is for the most part unbeliev-able. Think about that for a moment in your own life—all progress prior to experience is for the most part unbeliev-able. So many incredible things have happened in the gen-eration in which we live that we do not think anything is unbelievable anymore.

Think just for a minute. If you had told your grandpar-ents that one day people would go on a spaceship to the moon, what do you think they would have said? They would have said, "We don't believe it, how can that be?" But remember, all progress prior to experience is for the most part unbelievable. And the reason they didn't believe it is because they hadn't experienced it.

> *"All progress prior to experience is for the most part unbelievable."*

If we told a person who had seen a grown chicken, but who had never seen an egg, that the chicken had come out of an egg like that, do you think they would have believed us? I don't think they would. I think they would say to us, "How can that be?" If we told a person who had never seen an airplane that people travel in airplanes that fly like birds, do you think they would believe us? I don't think they would. At the beginning of this century people thought the Wright brothers were absolutely foolish because they said that one day people would travel by air as routinely as they travel by a train or a ship. All progress prior to experience is for the most part unbelievable.

Several years ago there was a newspaper story about a native tribe discovered in the Philippines that knew nothing about civilization. The people who found them—the language experts, the anthropologists, the psychologists, and the sociologists—said they lived in a culture that was equivalent to a culture of five thousand years ago. How would we like to explain to those natives found in the Philippines how you get light in a dark room by flipping a switch on the wall? How would we like to explain to those natives how we get water out of a faucet into a basin, and not only cold water, but also hot water—both cold and hot from the same spigot. Try to explain any modern invention to a native who lives in a five-thousand-year-old culture. Try to explain to those natives how a color television set works. Try to explain to them that two teams are playing a football game in New York, but you are watching it in your living room in Dallas. Try to explain to them how a telephone works. All progress prior to experience is for the most part unbelievable.

We take all of these things for granted because we live with them every day and we understand them. Therefore they are not nonsense to us because we have experienced them. We know they work. Is it then too incredible to believe that God so loved the world that he gave his only Son that whosoever believes in him should not perish but have eternal life in God? Is that too incredible to believe? I don't think so because God loves us and because God cares about us. Easter proclaims good news about people.

> ## "Easter proclaims good news about the future."

One of our most famous scientists said several years ago:

Science has found nothing that can disappear without a trace. Nature does not know extinction. All nature knows is transformation. If God applies this fundamental rule to the most insignificant part of this universe, surely it makes sense to assume that God applies it to the masterpiece of his creation, the human soul. Everything science has taught me, and continues to teach me, strengthens my belief that there is spiritual existence after physical death.

(Wernher von Braun)

It is impossible to speak about death without touching those who have recently lost loved ones or are facing that loss in the near future. One day all of us must walk through the valley of the shadow of death. Most of us realize that we do not speak easily about death. Because we do not speak easily about it, it may come as a stranger to us, leaving us confused, perplexed, perhaps even resentful. The time for God's people to consider their feelings toward death and their Christian understanding of death is not at the moment of death, but before death.

In a deep and profound sense, only one who has learned to die has really learned to live. And only one who has come face to face with the reality of death can come to grips with the reality of life. The quality of a person's life may also be found in the manner in which that person faces death. For in the facing of death one also learns how to face life; one begins to make decisions about what is really important in life. The tragedy is that most of us spend more time making preparations for a two-week vacation than we do in preparing ourselves for eternal life with God.

The story is told of a woman of great faith who went about in her community doing good and showing love and concern in all that she did. She was loved by all with whom she came in contact and her name became synonymous with faith and hope and love. She had many friends in various walks of life. One day she became ill and was taken to the hospital. Following extensive tests it was determined that she was terminally ill and probably would never leave the hospital. She wrote these words to her friends from her hospital bed:

> Dear Ones,
> To my surprise I have just been told that my days and hours are numbered. It may be that before this reaches you I shall have gone to the Palace to meet the King. Don't trouble to write. We shall meet in the morning!

"Where now, O death, is your victory; where now is your stinging power? . . . All thanks to God, then, who gives us the victory over these things through our Lord Jesus Christ!" (1 Cor. 15:55-57 JBP).

One of our great church historians, Stephen Neal, put it this way, "History shows us again and again that when everything seems to be darkest God has in the most unexpected way caused new light to shine in the darkness." This is what God did for us in the darkness of Calvary. God caused a new light to shine on Easter morning in the resurrection.

On February 27, 1991, Ruth Dillow was at her home in Chanute, Kansas, when she received the tragic news from the Pentagon that her son, Private First Class Clayton Carpenter, had stepped on a land mine during the Persian Gulf War and was killed. Such a moment of reality must be terrible for one who hears the news. Our hearts go out to all who experience such a tragedy. But three days later, Ruth Dillow received another telephone call. The voice on the other end said, "Mom, it's Clayton, I'm alive!" Ruth said that at first she could not believe it was the voice of her twenty-year-old son for whom she had mourned for three days. She said, "I just jumped up and down. I was overjoyed. I couldn't believe it."

But this morning we can believe it. For this morning our joy, too, is complete. Today and every day our Lord says to us, "I'm alive! And because I live, you shall live also." He is King of kings, and Lord of lords. Hallelujah! Hallelujah! The Lord omnipotent reigns forever and ever. Amen.

> *But on the first day of the week, at early dawn, they came to the tomb, taking the spices that they had prepared. They found the stone rolled away from the tomb, but when they went in, they did not find the body. While they were perplexed about this, suddenly two men in dazzling clothes stood beside them. The women were terrified and bowed their faces to the ground, but the men said to them, "Why do you look for the living among the dead? He is not here, but has risen."*
> *(Luke 24:1-5)*

"He is not here, but has risen."

When the Sabbath was over, just as the first day of the week was dawning, Mary from Magdala and the other Mary went to the tomb where Jesus' body had been laid. At that moment there was a great earthquake, for an angel of the Lord came down from heaven and rolled back the stone that was in front of the tomb. His appearance was dazzling, like lightning, and his clothes were as white as snow. The angel spoke to the women, "Do not be afraid. I know that you are looking for Jesus who was crucified. He is not here— he has been raised" (Matt. 28:5 JBP).

In the early days of the Christian church, as new converts became part of the Christian faith and the religion spread across the Roman Empire, the early Christians had a greeting for one another. Just as I might say to you, "Good morning," and you would reply, "Good morning to you," their greeting was "He is risen," to which the other replied, "He is risen, indeed!"

"He is not here, but has risen!" Those seven words have changed the course of history in our world.

Let's go back to Good Friday. As we read the Gospel stories of the crucifixion of Jesus, we see that almost all the disciples of Jesus deserted him when faced with the apparent disaster of the cross. With their leader dead and their hopes in shambles, they found themselves living in considerable apprehension. They were feeling helpless and hopeless, discouraged and disillusioned, empty in heart and broken in spirit. Life for them seemed to come to an end. The light had gone out of their hope. There seemed to be no tomorrow for them. Three years with Jesus, three years of following him, three years of being his disciples, and now they had to try to understand his stunning death and the numbing fact that Jesus was gone forever.

As we look at them we see a poor bedraggled band going home because their dreams had evaporated, going home because they were afraid for their lives. They had believed that Christ was to be the herald of a new order, but now it was evident that they had been wrong, for he had been crucified. In that bleak moment it looked as if the disciples were beaten. What is more striking is the remark of one of the disappointed disciples who said, "We had hoped that he was the one to redeem Israel" (Luke 24:21). And you can almost hear the next sentence, "But we guess we must have been wrong." The enthusiasm of his presence, the shared vitality, the creative hope—all these were gone. One more bubble had burst, one more hope had disappeared.

Yet within a very short time these very same disciples, this bedraggled little band, this discouraged and disillusioned group, suddenly became changed persons. They suddenly became persons filled with an extraordinary courage and spiritual strength that enabled them to defy the power of both religious and Roman authorities. They had come out of the slough of despondency and became triumphant and courageous persons proclaiming their faith.

> *"The broken disciples became strong and confident and bold as lions."*

What made the difference? "He is not here, but has risen!" That made the difference. The broken disciples became strong and confident and bold as lions. They now knew that God had made Christ stronger than those who sought to silence him. They sang, they rejoiced, they healed, they taught, they preached, they lived triumphantly. And they did not do these things for only a few days of passing enthusiasm after the resurrection of Christ, but they did them for the rest of their lives. They faced persecution and even death with a triumphant spirit that baffled their tormentors.

Why? Because "he is not here, but has risen."

But it took more than just an *event* for this to occur. Just observing the *event* of the resurrection was not enough to turn discouraged disciples into messengers of hope, or to convert disillusioned disciples into proclaimers of the Christian faith. It took more than an event—it took a personal experience with the risen Christ. The *event* had to become an *experience* in order for their lives to be changed. They could witness the event, but only as they had an experience with the living Christ did any change come to the disciples.

> ### "I was trying to make my faith fit into my education."

My early days in the Christian faith were probably very much like your early days in the Christian faith. I had a hard time understanding and believing in the resurrection of Christ. I was educated. I was trying to make my faith fit into my education. I asked, "How can a person who is dead live again? It doesn't make sense."

One day as I was studying the scripture and thinking about this question, I saw that the primary evidence offered by the apostles was not what they said, it is what they became because of the resurrection. The resurrection has to be for us more than an *event*; it has to be an *experience* with the living Christ. And to the apostles, what happened was not only that they said Christ had risen, but also that he had become alive in their hearts. They had an *experience* with the living Christ.

Look for a moment at the early church. The statistics did not seem to indicate a strong future for the church of Jesus Christ in Jerusalem that Friday night after the crucifixion. The administrative board (the disciples) had run away in panic, including all the male members; only a handful of women members remained. The treasurer, Judas, had run off with all the money. The church had no trustees, no property, no building, no budget, no staff, and no program. The civic authorities had labeled the followers of Jesus as dangerous persons. The founder had been executed as a common criminal. The early Christian church had no right to succeed, but it did. Why? Because "he is not here, but has risen!"

> *"The church had no trustees, no property, no building, no budget, no staff, and no program."*

A classic account of what happened to the early church is recorded for us in the book of Acts. The members of the Sanhedrin were perplexed with the teaching of Christ by the disciples. They felt it was disturbing the people.

> And when they had called in the apostles, they had them flogged. Then they ordered them not to speak in the name of Jesus, and let them go. As they left the council, they rejoiced that they were considered worthy to suffer dishonor for the sake of the name. And every day in the temple and at home they did not cease to teach and proclaim Jesus as the Messiah.
>
> (Acts 5:40-42)

What caused this change in the early disciples from the befuddled, bedraggled little group of disciples who had lost all hope, to those who defied not only the Roman authorities but also those in religious authority? I know of no other answer than that "he is not here, but has risen."

Some of the early Christians were thrown to the lions; some were attacked by gladiators; some were dipped into tar, tied to trees, and set on fire because of their Christian faith. Yet, in three centuries this motley group of early Christians had overcome the great Roman Empire and Christianity was flourishing around the world. I know of no answer that would have enabled the early church to sustain itself in the midst of such adversity but the fact that "he is not here, but has risen." That sustained the early disciples and the early church.

But the real question that we face this morning is, "What does this Easter mean to us?" We have gathered today to celebrate the Easter event, the resurrection of Christ. Yet, it will be hollow mockery if that is the only reason we have come. We are here today, also, to renew our own experience with the living Christ. For us, too, the event must become an experience. We celebrate an event that occurred at a particular time in history. But Easter becomes a reality only when it leads us to a continuing experience with the living Lord.

As Christians we say we trust God; we say we believe in the love of God. Are we then to think that God is either so powerless to renew the life that he first created or so lacking in concern for us that his last word to his faithful children is the everlasting night of nothingness? I do not believe that. I believe that the God who loves us and the God who has created us with the yearning for immortality will not betray us in our quest for that immortality. I believe that the God who created human personality can and will preserve that personality. There will be that sense of fulfillment.

> *"When death comes, we shall not be on an uncharted journey."*

Jesus said, "I am the resurrection and the life. Those who believe in me, even though they die, will live" (John 11:25). Is this a hollow promise that God made through Christ to us? I do not believe it is a hollow promise; I believe it is a true promise. And Paul assured us, "But in fact Christ has been raised from the dead. . . . For since death came through a human being, the resurrection of the dead has also come through a human being; for as all die in Adam, so all will be made alive in Christ" (1 Cor. 15:20, 21-22).

The resurrection of Jesus Christ is our faith for today and our hope for tomorrow. It is the assurance that we have a living Savior to help us live as we ought to live. And it is our assurance that when death comes, we shall not be on an uncharted journey, but on a planned trip that goes from life to death to life eternal with God.

The mother of one of our members was confined to a bed in a nursing home. She was ill, and there were times when she became overwrought. In order to keep the mother from falling out of the bed she was kept strapped in. Above the bed was a sign that read, "This patient must be restrained at all times." The daughter said this broke her heart. And every time the daughter went to see her mother she cried as her mother asked her to be released so that she might be free from the bondage of the bed. The mother died. The daughter said the first thing she did when her mother died was to walk into that room, take the sign off the wall, tear it up, throw it away, and say, "Thank God, she is free at last!"

That is what our Christian faith says to us about death— thank God, we are free at last. We have no fear of death. Death holds no fear for the Christian. Because Christ lives, we live also. What we celebrate in the Easter Resurrection is a victory over the grave, a victory over death. It is the sovereign power of God that we celebrate, a power that was released to us through God's gift of life in the risen Christ. Easter calls us to affirm our faith in the power of the Resurrection.

I had a friend who died at an all-too-young age. I saw him often during the last days of his life. He was a strong

Christian, one who understood about life and death. I went to strengthen him. But I came away every single time strengthened by his faith in the living God. He died as he had lived—with patience and love and submission in his heart, with the simple faith of a trusting child, and with the superb gallantry of a great soul who had gone home to be with God. "He is not here, but has risen." That is our Easter faith.

The story is told that Queen Victoria went to the Albert Hall in London to hear the *Messiah* sung. She listened as the majestic words and music soared through that great hall: "Blessing and honor, glory and power, be unto to him that sitteth upon the throne, and unto the Lamb, forever and ever." As Handel's great oratorio reached its mighty climax and the strains of the immortal music died away, the queen stood in the royal box, and although she was not supposed to give any sign of approval or disapproval, she bore this testimony before the hushed audience, "I take the crown of all Britain and put it at the feet of my Savior, and still I am an unprofitable soul."

"He is not here, but has risen!" He is King of kings and Lord of lords. Hallelujah! Hallelujah! The Lord God omnipotent reigns forever and ever. Amen.